Race Mixing in the Public Schools

Charles V. Willie
with Jerome Beker

The Praeger Special Studies program—utilizing the most modern and efficient book production techniques and a selective worldwide distribution network—makes available to the academic, government, and business communities significant, timely research in U.S. and international economic, social, and political development.

Race Mixing in the Public Schools

PRAEGER SPECIAL STUDIES IN U.S. ECONOMIC, SOCIAL, AND POLITICAL ISSUES

Praeger Publishers   New York   Washington   London

Library of Congress Cataloging in Publication Data

Willie, Charles Vert, 1927-
    Race mixing in the public schools.

    (Praeger special studies in U.S. economic,
social, and political issues)
        1. School integration—United States.
2. Students' socioeconomic status—United States.
3. Students—United States—Conduct of life.
I. Beker, Jerome, joint author.   II. Title.
LA229. W53   370. 19'342   73-10947

PRAEGER PUBLISHERS
111 Fourth Avenue, New York, N.Y. 10003, U.S.A.
5, Cromwell Place, London SW7 2JL, England

Published in the United States of America in 1973
by Praeger Publishers, Inc.

With hope
this book is dedicated to

Sarah Susannah, Martin Charles, James Theodore
and the children of their generation

This study was financed by a grant from the U.S. Office of Education: Project No. D-125 and Contract No. OE-5-10-117. The National Institute of Mental Health also contributed through a grant: No. R11-MH-1652. The grants were awarded to Jerome Beker and the Youth Development Center at Syracuse University and are acknowledged with thanks and appreciation. The information presented herein has emerged from the research of the authors and does not necessarily represent official policy of the sponsoring agencies.

The purpose of the study was to discover patterns of social adjustment of young people who were transferred to a school outside their neighborhood. A considerable amount of research has been conducted on the academic adjustment of such children; little is known of their social adjustment. We hold the view that both academic and social adjustment are significant.

The name of the community is fictitious, as are the names of the schools, principals, teachers, and children. Their experiences are real, and they constitute an important report of turbulent times of personal adaptation and institutional change in America.

Acknowledged with appreciation is the assistance of Dr. Richard O. Hope and Dr. Robert La Porte, Jr., who were research assistants to the senior author at the time this study was conducted. The skillful editorial assistance rendered by Dorothy Sickels and the typing preparation of the manuscript by Jane Frost and Mary Walsh also are gratefully appreciated. Tables of supporting data are in the Appendix, to which the interested reader may refer.

CONTENTS

LIST OF APPENDIX TABLES

x

Race Mixing in
the Public Schools

In the considered opinion of John Seeley and his associates, "public education has become one of the most important socializing agents [in countries such as the United States and Canada]" (Seeley et al., 1956, p. 226). This idea is also embraced by others, David Goslin states that "the school plays a major role . . . in helping children learn to control their emotions, to deal with as well as assume positions of authority, and to recognize the existence of status hierarchies in social groups" (Goslin 1965, p. 5). Although James Coleman, senior author of the national study Equality of Educational Opportunity (Coleman et al., 1966), enters a cautionary note about the relative influence of the school over and against that of the home upon achievement, he nevertheless asserts that "the variation in achievement of different children within a school is not a result wholly of what the children bring to the school," that there are interactions between the characteristics of children and the opportunities provided for them in the school (Coleman 1968, p. 20). Coleman concludes, on the basis of his study, that "there are three major places in which a child can find educational resources necessary to his achievement, the home, the environment provided by his peers in school and neighborhood, and the resources provided by the school itself" (Coleman 1968, p. 24).

This book will examine the effects of neighborhood location, the educational context of the school, and such family characteristics as race and socioeconomic status upon the social adjustment of children who are part of a program deliberately designed to achieve greater racial integration.

The coming together of children of disparate social and educational backgrounds is likely to cause some psychological trauma. With reference to the integration of children with differing achievement levels, however, "the evidence indicates that such psychological discomforts are not lasting" (Coleman 1968, p. 25). Indeed there are positive benefits, mentioned by Coleman but seldom acknowledged in the public debate about the assets and liabilities of race mixing in the public schools. He states that "Negro children in an integrated school come to gain a greater sense of their efficacy to control their destiny. It is very likely due to the fact that they see that they can do some things better than whites and can perform in school better than some whites, a knowledge which they never had so long as they were isolated in an all-black school" (Coleman 1968, p. 25).

An important part of the story about race mixing in the public schools has been the adaptability and courage exhibited by both black and white children. The difficulties and disorders have been recorded and preserved as public information. But the quiet courage of these students has been ignored, except in the writings of Robert Coles and a few other observers. In her book entitled The Long Shadow of Little Rock (1962), Daisy Bates tells about the courageous behavior of Elizabeth Eckford, one of the black students who integrated Little Rock's Central High School in 1957. On what was to be the first day of class, Elizabeth boarded a bus alone en route to school. She got off a block away from the building, saw a large crowd, but proceeded to walk toward the front entrance. The crowd shouted and moved in close; some spat at her. Someone yelled, "Lynch her, lynch her!" Elizabeth said afterwards, "I wasn't too scared because all the time I kept thinking the guards would protect me." When she finally reached the front entrance to the school, Elizabeth discovered that the guards were there with bayonets—not to protect her but to keep her out. At that point she became nearly hysterical and ran toward a bench at a bus stop; there she was befriended by only one white man and one white woman as the angry crowd surged closer, shouting hostilities. Eventually she boarded a bus and narrowly escaped. Later the Arkansas National Guard was federalized and ordered to permit the integration of Central High School as well as to protect all of the students, including the blacks. Despite the memory of a threatening mob, Elizabeth returned, became a matriculating student, and graduated from Central High School in 1960 (Bates 1969, pp. 203-206). Coles has recorded moving stories of courageous white families who kept their children in integrated schools in defiance of threats from the mob and its attempt to enforce a boycott of such schools by whites (Coles 1968, pp. 274-280).

Indeed, the children who have participated in this era of dramatic cultural change, especially the change in the racial composition of public school student bodies, have been "children of crisis." A crisis, of course, is a turning point. In every innovation, there is the possibility of enhancement and degeneration. With reference to social and psychological adjustment, the crisis apparently has strengthened many youths. Aaron Lipton said of black and white pupilts in Hartsdale, New York, "The children in our school district have been going to school together for a long time. They were able to see that they were not so different from one another. They were able to see that they could learn from one another" (Lipton 1968, p. 223). In learning how to get along with each other, the black and white children in the public schools have developed some important social skills. Eventually these skills could prove as important as the academic skills that we usually measure.

According to Thomas Pettigrew, "however important, high achievement-test scores are surely not the sole goal of education." Pettigrew states that many advocates of integrated education tend to argue their case only in terms of the nonacademic benefits. He reviews several studies which demonstrate that people who are educated in interracial settings tend to continue interracial relationships even into adulthood. On the basis of these studies, "It appears . . . that desegregated schooling does in fact prepare its products—both blacks and whites—for interracial living as adults" (Pettigrew 1971, pp. 64-65).

Beyond any moral or social consequence, race mixing in the public schools has educational outcomes, one of which is the possibility of cross-racial self-evaluation. We have already seen that Coleman mentions this as an advantage for blacks. Pettigrew offers the hypothesis that it is of benefit to both blacks and whites (Pettigrew 1971, p. 66). One of America's most distinguished educators, Benjamin Mays, tells us that his matriculation at Bates College, which is predominantly white, was the experience which dismissed from his mind for all time the myth of the inherent superiority of whites. Mays said that he had objective proof through the competitive experience that he, although black, "had done better in academic performances, in public speaking, and in argumentation and debate than the vast majority of [his] classmates" (Mays 1971, p. 60).

It is quite possible that the opportunity for cross-racial self-evaluation has dismissed for all time in the minds of some whites the myth of the inherent inferiority of blacks. This new learning by direct experience is possible in a racially mixed school. For example, a study of black students in four predominantly white colleges in New York State revealed that the proportion of black seniors with self-reported cumulative grade averages of B and above was higher than the proportion of whites with similar grade averages, although freshman, sophomore, and junior blacks had fewer high achievers compared with whites (Willie and McCord 1972, p. 87). Whites who have had little or no contact with blacks may disbelieve this finding. There are many possible explanations; but the explanation is not so important as are the actual research data that some blacks clearly have the capacity to overachieve whites academically.

Black and white children who have lived through the crisis years of race mixing in the public schools have developed more realistic self-concepts. This, then, is a psychological outcome of integration. In 1940-41 when Kenneth and Mamie Clark analyzed the genesis and development of racial identification as a function of ego development, they found in an experiment that a majority of black children preferred a white doll to a brown doll. The Clarks interpreted the choice as a negation or rejection of the brown doll. They buttressed their argument with statements from the black children concerning why they did not choose the brown doll: "He's ugly," or "it don't look pretty," or "him black," or "got black on him" (Clark and Clark 1947, pp. 169-178).

Today, several decades beyond the period of officially sanctioned segregation when the Clarks conducted their experiments and beyond the street demonstrations of the mid-twentieth century civil rights movement, some blacks still may prefer skin coloring lighter than their own. But this preference is now more likely to be a result of the internalization of the mass culture of a predominantly white society than a negation or rejection of their own race. As Gloria Johnson Powell has pointed out, "Self-awareness does not emerge in an all-or-none fashion" (Powell 1973, pp. 299-318). Thus we should not be surprised to discover that the preference of some blacks for a lighter skin coloring may still be due, in part, to rejection of their race, but this is probably true to a lesser degree than it was in the past.

While the Clarks' study appeared to indicate that blacks had a negative concept of themselves and therefore preferred persons with characteristics unlike their own, recent studies, one of which is reported by Powell, have found that the average self-concept score for black children is higher than the average self-concept score for white children (Powell 1973, pp. 299-318). The higher self-concept for blacks is probably due on the one hand to the action generated during the civil rights movement and the continuing press for liberation, and on the other hand to the increased opportunity for cross-racial self-evaluation made possible by school desegregation.

Compared with the information we have on the self-concepts of blacks, there is little systematically gathered information on changes which have taken place over the years in self-concepts of whites. My guess is that there is less of an inclination now for whites to accept a position of dominance as a natural right. Certainly the May 17, 1954, Supreme Court decision outlawing enforced segregation in the public schools was a sign that whatever comfort whites may have derived from limiting their association in school to members of their own race was not as important to the nation as extending the Constitutional principle of "equal protection of the laws" to all. The unanimous decision of the Supreme Court in Brown v. Board of Education demonstrated this fact.

In the mid-1960s, during the early days of desegregated education in the State of Alabama, two social scientists studied a sample of the black children attending desegregated junior high and senior high schools in 23 counties. The black students were asked whether they felt the white students changed in their relationship to blacks during the course of the year. Almost 80 percent said that "whites did change somewhat" (Chesler and Segal 1968, p. 27).

And so the times are changing. In the light of the changing relationships required by law, whites probably are less able to impute inferiority to blacks but may not yet be able to give up their claim to racial superiority. Perry Morgan, in an essay entitled "The Case for the White Southerner," admits that the Southern heritage is gone, but he is quick to say that it is not forgotten (Morgan 1964, p. 147). We may probably extend this statement to apply to whites in all sections of the nation. The heritage of exclusion is gone but not forgotten. Because this book presents data on white teachers as well as white students, it will provide an opportunity to examine differences, if there are any, between white youngsters and white adults in their attachment to the concept of white supremacy and white exclusivity.

From a social science perspective, such an analysis could be fruitful in shedding light on the mutual misunderstanding which is said to exist between adults and young people as well as between blacks and whites. Most of us, including parents, teachers, and students, probably look first within ourselves for a hint or indication of what others think. Gordon Allport, however, has cautioned us to "guard against the fallacy of projection: of assuming that other people have states of mind, interests, and values precisely like our own" (Allport 1955, p. 23). An excellent example of the mutual misunderstandings to which projection can lead is the following exchange between Robert Coles, the psychiatrist, and a black minister, concerning the Moynihan Report on the black family (1965). This is what they said:

Coles:	"The Moynihan Report was a call for action."
Minister:	"It was a call to white people. It did not speak to Negroes."
Coles:	"I disagree. It spoke to Americans. It was written by a politician, in the best sense of the word; in your sense of a good politician. He wanted change, or action."
Minister:	"You don't see how we feel, reading those headlines, about our badness, our weakness— again."
Coles:	"I disagree. I see how you feel, but I guess I can't feel as you do. We keep on coming back to that."

Minister: "Yes. We do; and all over the country people
             will, for a long while, I think."
                                        (Coles 1969, pp. 145-146)

    White and black social scientists experience this problem too;
members of each racial group tend to examine different aspects of
the black way of life, presumably based upon what they consider to be
important. We have observed, for example, that "many white scholars
are more interested in studying the weaknesses in the black family
and factors associated with its breakdown, while many black scholars
are more interested in studying the strengths in the black family and
factors associated with its stability." But "an adequate sociology of
black family life requires studies of strengths and weaknesses" (Willie
1973, p. 1,271).
    The same point may be made about teachers and students. They
look at the educational process from different perspectives, each pro-
jecting his or her own idea of what is important upon others. The
teacher is concerned with producing a socially desirable adult (Peterson 1962, p. 134), while the student is concerned with obtaining a
relevant education. Relevancy is defined by one black college student
as "anything which has to do with me" (Willie and McCord 1972, p.
46). This definition, of course, is quite subjective. Since both the
teacher and the student, like others in society, tend to look first within themselves for an indication of what is going on in others, it is all
the more important to ask others to speak for themselves as a correc-
tive for the mutual misperceptions that are likely to flow from our
faulty projections. In this book, black and white students will speak
for themselves concerning their social and emotional adaptations to
school; their statements will then be compared with the assessments
of their teachers.
    In addition to investigating the adaptation of individuals, we will
look at the circumstances and conditions of school integration itself.
We will focus on the context within which children of differing racial,
socioeconomic, and residential neighborhood backgrounds do or do
not integrate. S. M. Miller and Pamela Roby state that "in the fifties
and early sixties the burden of desegregating American society was
left to children and the educational arena rather than to adults who
were wary of the task they displaced to their offspring." They go on
to say that the schools have made obvious and important contributions
"but they cannot be assigned the entire burden of reforming the social
structure" (Miller and Roby 1968, p. 18). There is much truth in this
observation. Yet it should not be assumed that the schools have
reached the limits of what they can do to further racial integration.
    For the schools to insist that they are only a minion of society
and can go no further than the local community is prepared to go is

6

a "cop-out." Already the schools have desegregated as much as or more than some other community institutions such as churches, synagogues, and voluntary associations. Robin Williams and Margaret Ryan, who supervised a study of the desegregation experience in 24 communities in six states, reached this conclusion based on their analyses of the field reports.

Public school desegregation or integration is only loosely correlated with the attitudes or prejudices of the population. Successful public school desegregation has been carried out in places where supposedly the prevailing attitudes favored segregation and where other institutions continued to be segregated. . . . Segregation [in public education] has persisted for years in other [communities] where attitudes were relatively favorable for integration. . . . In some [communities] . . . school desegregation was successful in a completely segregated environment. [Williams and Ryan 1954, pp. 240-241]

In his prize-winning book People in Context, George Stern elaborates upon the concept of "environmental press," which includes conditions that represent impediments to a [personal] need "as well as [conditions] that are likely to facilitate its expression. These conditions, which establish what is commonly referred to as the climate or atmosphere of an institution, are to be found in the structure created or tolerated by others. The components of this structure may be physical as well as social. . . . " (Stern 1970, p. 7).

The American society has tried to shift the burden of desegregation to the schools, and the schools have tried to shift the burden of integration to the students. Ultimately these approaches cannot work. While there is much the schools can do on their own, with or without community support, they will ultimately require fiscal aid to institute a busing program that will counteract the racial and socioeconomic homogeneity of students who live in the vicinity of a particular school. Also, schools with heterogeneous student bodies need sufficient resources to reduce the size of classes so that they can institute individualized programs of instruction in reading, mathematics, and the language arts.

In the end, students need strong staff leaders who have a strong sense of identity with and loyalty to education as a free enterprise. Indeed, there is an interaction between the executive professional leadership shown by the principal, the morale of teachers, their professional performance, and the academic performance of students (Gross and Herriott 1965, pp. 34-57). Moreover, when conflicts do occur between one student and another, as they will, the

7

school needs professional staff who have the judgment and wisdom "to let them talk and to find out what they have to say." In short, the school needs professional leaders who permeate the institution with an attitude of fairness (Lipton 1968, pp. 224-225).

It is important to examine the bases for success and failure in integrated education, as we will in this book. The effort is timely and the objective is still the same—the achievement of quality education through diversification. As Pettigrew points out, "Integration has not failed in America, for it still remains to be tried as a national policy. . . . [Thus far] the nation has failed integration" (Pettigrew 1971, p. 297). The findings we present should help the nation to pick itself up, dust itself off, and start all over again.

REFERENCES

Allport, Gordon W. Becoming: Basic Considerations for a Psychology
1955   of Personality. New Haven: Yale University Press.

Bailey, Kenneth K. Southern White Protestantism in the Twentieth
1964   Century. New York: Harper and Row.

Bates, Daisy. The Long Shadow of Little Rock. New York: David
1962   McKay.

Bates, Daisy. "The Long Shadow of Little Rock," in Jay David, ed.,
1969   Growing Up Black. New York: Pocket Books.

Chesler, Mark, and Phyllis Segal. "Southern Negroes' Initial Experi-
1968   ences and Reactions in School Desegregation." Integrated
         Education, Volume 6, Number 1 (Jan. -Feb.).

Clark, Kenneth B., and Mamie P. Clark. "Racial Identification and
1947   Preference in Negro Children," in Theodore M. Newcomb
         and Eugene L. Hartley, Readings in Social Psychology. New
         York: Henry Holt and Company.

Coleman, James S. "Equality of Educational Opportunity." Integrated
1968   Education, Volume 6, Number 5 (Sept.-Oct.)

Coleman, James S., et al. Equality of Educational Opportunity.
1966   Washington, D.C.: U.S. Government Printing Office.

Coles, Robert. Children of Crisis. New York: Dell Publishing
1968   Company.

Goslin, David A. The School in Contemporary Society. Chicago:
1965   Scott, Foresman and Company.

Gross, Neal, and Robert E. Herriott. Staff Leadership in Public
1965   Schools: A Sociological Inquiry. New York: John Wiley
        and Sons.

Lipton, Aaron. "Day-to-Day Problems of School Integration," in
1968   Meyer Weinberg, Integrated Education—a Reader. Beverly
        Hills: The Glencoe Press.

Mays, Benjamin E. Born to Rebel. New York: Charles Scribner's
1971   Sons.

Miller, S. M., and Pamela Roby, "Education and Redistribution: The
1968   Limits of a Strategy." Integrated Education, Volume 6,
        Number 5 (Sept.-Oct.).

Morgan, Perry. "The Case for the White Southerner," in Hubert
1964   H. Humphrey, ed., School Desegregation. New York:
        T. Y. Crowell, p. 140-50.

Peterson, A. D. C. A Hundred Years of Education. New York:
1962   Collier.

Pettigrew, Thomas F. Racially Separate or Together? New York:
1971   McGraw-Hill Book Company.

Powell, Gloria Johnson. "Self-Concept in White and Black Children,"
1973   in Charles V. Willie, Bernard Kramer, Bertram S. Brown,
        eds., Racism and Mental Health. Pittsburgh: University
        of Pittsburgh Press.

Seeley, John R., Alexander Sim, and Elizabeth W. Loosley Crest-
1956   wood Heights. New York: Basic Books.

Stern, George G. People in Context. New York: John Wiley and
1970   Sons.

U.S. Department of Labor. The Negro Family: A Case for National
1965   Action. Washington D.C.: U.S. Government Printing Office.

Williams, Robin M., and Margaret W. Ryan. Schools in Transition.
1954   Chapel Hill: The University of North Carolina Press.

Willie, Charles V. "On Merton's 'Insiders and Outsiders'," American
  1973   Journal of Sociology, Volume 78, Number 5 (March).

Willie, Charles V., and Arline Sakuma McCord. Black Students at
  1972   White Colleges. New York: Praeger.

The problems of integration and busing are prominent today in the minds of Americans, both black and white. However, they have seldom been studied dispassionately from all angles. For instance, the social adjustment of a child moved to a new school to alleviate overcrowding at his old school is too often overlooked. The reactions of the teachers, the principal, and the parents all enter into the picture. Our major goal in this book is to help gain a clearer understanding of what is happening to the children who have become pioneers in an era of social change.

Because we firmly believe that schools must be concerned about the whole person, we chose to focus our research on the patterns of social adjustment experienced by elementary and junior high school students who were assigned to new schools for the purpose of achieving a better racial balance. We wanted to determine whether our findings about newly bused children reflected the attitudes of the neighborhoods from which they came and their personal characteristics, or merely the fact of their newness to the school. We therefore obtained comparable information from new children in the same school who were not bused in but were attending their own neighborhood school. These data facilitated a comparative analysis.

We were most fortunate in uncovering a situation in a northern city, Centralia, that illustrated in four of its schools—two elementary and two junior high schools—many of the integration problems facing the entire nation. Realizing the diverse and often emotional factors involved, we decided to go into the matter in depth. Trained observers were placed directly in the classrooms, always with the permission of the school authorities. Some observers stayed in the one school for the entire year, recording the reactions of students, teachers, parents, and principals. Their findings, often quoted word for word in subsequent chapters, are not only enlightening—they are fascinating. The final two chapters recapitulate the findings and discuss more specifically the methods used. We will constantly try to review the various problems of social integration from the point of view of young and old, professional and nonprofessional.

Before we come to the specific findings, however, it will be necessary to give the community background so essential to a complete understanding of the complex situations. It is, in fact, interesting to see the citywide reaction to segregation. The names of the city, the schools, and all personnel involved are fictitious. The situations nonetheless are very real.

Centralia is a middle-sized city with a population of approximately 250,000, and is the central city of a county metropolitan area with a population of about 500,000, including city and noncity residents. It is an industrial center with more than 500 manufacturing plants in and around the city. Centralia is also an educational center, with several public and private colleges.

The small black population rapidly increased from about 2 percent to about 6 or 7 percent during the 1950s, and now makes up about one-tenth of the total city population. The black ghetto in the center of the city was crowded and housing was substandard. The frustrations caused by racial segregation and discrimination had been unchanneled in the past, but protest groups such as The Congress for Racial Equality (CORE) were forming during the 1960s.

In the spring of 1962, the principal of Spring Street Elementary School in Centralia requested that the Research Department of the Centralia School District develop a plan to alleviate overcrowding at his school. This was a routine request. The Centralia School District was committed to the neighborhood school concept. The Research Department usually met such requests by adjusting boundaries between two or more schools. Since each school was located in the center of the residential area from which its students came, overcrowding at one school was usually handled by shifting the children who lived on the periphery of that area to another school where more space was available. Since adjustments were made with children who lived on the periphery, these youngsters traveled about the same distance to the new school as to the old school. Thus the neighborhood school concept was retained.

The Research Department recommended that students who lived near the southern boundary of the Spring Street district enroll in the Simpson Elementary School. Unlike similar recommendations in the past, which were routinely approved by the School Board as submitted by the school superintendent, this one was tabled and eventually rejected.

The reason for rejecting the proposal was the storm of community controversy that followed its presentation. The controversy had to do with the racial balance of some Centralia public schools. Spring Street Elementary School is located on the periphery of the black ghetto; several black families had moved into the Spring Street district, and its student body was about 30 percent nonwhite. The Spring Street Mothers Club and several community associations protested that the children to be transferred out of the Spring Street district were white and that further reduction in the population of white children in their school would result in a serious racial imbalance. The proposal of the Research Department would decrease the number of children at the crowded Spring Street school but increase the proportion of black youngsters. The community groups insisted that they liked the racial composition of their school as it was and wanted to keep it that way.

The School Board, while rejecting the staff recommendation that would have decreased the proportion of white students in Spring Street, would not formally acknowledge the race of students as a legitimate factor in defining school boundaries.

CORE, reacting to the School Board's reluctance to acknowledge race as a legitimate consideration, broadened the issue to a citywide attack upon de facto segregated schools. The School Board refused to negotiate with CORE or any other community group about the racial composition of school populations. In general, the School Board and staff took the position that they should be "colorblind" in dealing with children. The protest groups, and particularly CORE, interpreted the School Board's position not as a commitment to racial justice but as a method of evading and as a way of discharging itself from any responsibility for the existence of racially segregated schools.

The School Board's failure to deal in a creative way with demands to eliminate segregated schools may have been due in part to the absence of a permanent leader of the staff. Following the resignation of one superintendent (for reasons unrelated to the Spring Street School issue), an acting superintendent was appointed who did not have the power to commit the school system to a long-term course of action. Even before this administrative state of limbo in staff direction, the School Board had given no indication that it was prepared to seek ways of eliminating racially segregated schools. The School Board pointed to segregated housing as contributing to the existing situation. Meanwhile, CORE pressed its proposal to deal with segregated schools "now."

When the School Board adamantly refused to entertain CORE's proposal, several protest groups picketed the headquarters of the Centralia School District and staged a boycott on the first day of school at one elementary school whose student population was about 90 percent black. Nearly 900 of the 1,100 pupils stayed at home. This was the first effective boycott ever carried out against the Centralia School District. The school system's reaction was a mixture of surprise and outrage. But the demonstration led to the formation of the Education Committee, which was convened under the auspices of the Centralia Area Council of the State Human Relations Commission. The committee was a kind of third party consisting of representatives of the School Board, the protest groups, and leading citizens at large; it was formed to discuss the CORE charges of the existence of segregated schools and to help find ways of solving the issue that had resulted in a disruption of the orderly opening of school. The Education Committee issued a report showing that school segregation did exist and requesting that the School Board issue a policy statement pertaining to its plans to improve racial balance in the Centralia schools.

A new superintendent then entered the picture. He did not have to defend past actions of the school staff and was therefore able to take a more flexible stance. He gained the trust of protest group leaders and members of the Board of Education and served as a channel of communication between the interested community groups, parents, and the School Board. In spite of the stance of the new superintendent and the work of the Education Committee of the State Human Relations Commission, it is doubtful that without pressure from outside the local community the School Board would have changed its firm position against recognizing race as a legitimate consideration in devising school boundaries.

A special message from the State Department of Education called upon all local school boards and superintendents to take immediate steps to solve problems of racial imbalance in specific school populations; a school was considered racially imbalanced if more than 50 percent of its students were nonwhite. The message further requested that local school boards report to the state educational agency their findings regarding racial imbalance and their efforts to solve this problem. The message has been varyingly called a "directive" or an "advisory"—in effect, it carried the weight of a directive.

With this message from the state as a primary stimulus, and with the findings of the local Education Committee to point to, the School Board was able to change from its position of ignoring race as a consideration in devising school boundaries to one of actively seeking a way to integrate schools in spite of segregated neighborhoods. The School Board could make this change without losing face since it was directed to do so by higher authority. The change was also facilitated by the recommendations of the new school superintendent.

The superintendent presented a case for racial integration that went beyond a simple appeal to the ideal of brotherhood. He constantly

14

emphasized that low-achieving students, meaning those who attended inner-city schools, could not be expected to improve themselves unless they were educated in the presence of high-achieving students. Indeed, one leader in education described the situation this way: "The black children . . . have a fixed level of failure that could be altered with the integration program. The schools must push social change."

The integration program proposed by the school superintendent was designed to change the racial composition of two elementary and two junior high schools. The three schools that had predominantly black student populations were to remain open, but some students in two of these schools would be bused to schools with lower proportions of blacks. It was also planned to shift some whites at the junior high school level who had formerly attended a combination elementary-junior high school into the predominantly black junior high school. The junior high section of the comibnation school was being phased out in keeping with a School Board policy of eliminating combination schools.

The official reasons for reassigning students were given at two School Board meetings. They included "improving racial balance;" but this was listed as only one among several reasons, such as reducing overcrowded schools, retiring obsolete buildings, re-establishing neighborhood schools, redefining neighborhood school boundaries, and providing increased flexibility for future reorganization.

The proposal to integrate a predominantly black inner-city junior high school was new and different. Plymouth, the combination school whose junior high division was being closed out, is located in an area which is one of the lowest in socioeconomic status.

The other three schools scheduled to receive black students were located in neighborhoods of above-average socioeconomic status. The elementary schools, Simpson and Highland, were located in respectively higher income areas; and the junior high school, Lincoln, was located in one of the highest. In general, the students in these schools were white and of Anglo-Saxon ancestry. The Lincoln Junior High School district also included part of a middle-class Jewish neighborhood. The schools from which black youngsters were transferred—Corliss Elementary, Denison Elementary, and Monroe Junior High—were all located in neighborhoods of below-average socioeconomic status.

Monroe occupied a unique position in the reassignment scheme; while it was scheduled to receive 200 white children, 75 black youngsters were to be transferred from Monroe to Lincoln Junior High School according to the original plans. About 60 first, second, and third graders were to be transported by bus from Corliss to Simpson Elementary School, and Highland Elementary School was scheduled to receive approximately 100 pupils from other schools in all six of its grade levels.

In the fall of 1964, Centralia launched its first major though modest effort to achieve racial balance in some of its public schools. The total number of pupils to be reassigned, approximately 435, was less than 2 percent of the more than 30,000 children attending public schools in the city. The School Board was supported in this move by such groups as the League of Women Voters and the City Human Relations Commission. Other groups opposed this modest beginning. One of the most vocal of these, a group of white parents of Plymouth children, publicly stated that they were opposed to the transfer because they favored the neighborhood school concept and because their children would be endangered by having to cross a major traffic artery to get to Monroe Junior High School. Privately, many Plymouth parents were opposed to sending their children to a school whose student population was predominantly black.

White parents both in lower-income and higher-income areas fixated on the neighborhood school concept as a reason for opposing the plan to bus students. However, some parents in the higher-income Simpson Elementary School district also opposed the transferring of grade-school youngsters from the inner city to Simpson because they were afraid that the overall level of achievement at the school would be lowered. Many white parents, however, actively supported the School Board's plan and visited some inner-city black families, urging parents to let their children participate in the new program. Parent-Teacher Associations in three of the "receiving" schools were not very vocal; they quietly sought explanations from the school superintendent and others. But the Simpson PTA polarized on the integration issue and has remained an organization of opposing factions.

In spite of the opposition, the School Board moved ahead with its plan. Its forward movement engendered more support. One concession was made, however; an open school policy was affirmed. This meant that children in one school district could apply for transfer to another school district if space was available in the other school. In some cities the open school policy has been used as a means of integrating children restricted to inner-city ghettoes into schools outside of the city center that are not used to capacity. In Centralia, the open school policy was used by parents to circumvent the planned reassignment of 200 Plymouth School white children to the predominantly black Monroe School. When school opened in September, only 31 white children from Plymouth, or from elementary schools that normally fed children to the junior high division of Plymouth, came to Monroe. (A total of 52 children came from the Plymouth district, but 21 of these children were nonwhite.) Many children assigned to Monroe made application during the summer to be transferred; these applications were acted upon favorably. Other children previously enrolled in other junior high schools but reassigned to Monroe did not get around to applying for a transfer from Monroe until after the fall school term had started. These applications also were acted upon favorably. Rather than contributing to integration, the open school policy fostered continued segregation, especially at Monroe.

Not only did Monroe Junior High School receive fewer whites than expected, it transferred fewer blacks to Lincoln Junior High School than the proposed plan called for. The final figures revealed that only about 30 blacks were transferred to Lincoln instead of 75. Thus the proportion of black children at Monroe remained between 75 and 80 percent before and after the transfers, which had been designed to affect the school's racial balance. Failure on the part of Monroe to transfer the proposed number of students was due in part to the principal's efforts to discourage transfers, and his informal invitation to school administrators, including the principal at Lincoln Junior High School, to return to Monroe any students who were trouble-makers. The principal's rationale for this behavior was his belief, as he put it, that the students liked Monroe better and should have the privilege of remaining or returning to the school they preferred. Actually the Monroe principal did not attempt to evade the racial integration intended in the transfer plan. A more pressing personal concern for him, one which took precedence over any schoolwide scheme to achieve racial balance, was the possibility that Monroe would be closed. The student bodies of several inner-city schools had been dwindling as a result of the stepped-up relocation accompanying an urban renewal clearance project which was being carried out in their districts. To justify the need to remain open, the principal of Monroe wanted to hold onto as many of the students as he could. Fewer students than expected had come from Plymouth to Monroe; had Monroe transferred to Lincoln the number of students called for, Monroe would have experienced a net decrease rather than the net increase in students anticipated in the original plan.

Some black families had moved out of the Monroe district into the Lincoln district because of urban renewal and relocation. So with the 30 children transferred from Monroe and with the new black children who had moved into the Lincoln district, Lincoln Junior High School began the school year with a student population that was 19 percent black.

The two elementary schools, Highland and Simpson, received nearly as many students as anticipated, although in all instances the totals were somewhat below those prescribed in the Board-approved plan. Fifty-two pupils (45 of whom were black) were transferred from Corliss to Simpson, and Highland received 80 pupils (59 of whom were black or American Indians). Thus Simpson began the year with a student body that was 2 percent black, and Highland began the year with a student body that was 18 percent black.

All this means that Centralia began its first efforts to achieve racial balance in a selected number of schools by deliberately reassigning approximately 230 students (see Tables 1 and 2 in the Appendix) rather than the 435 called for in the original plan. Of the total number of reassigned students, only about 165 were black (see Table 3). This means that the great hue and cry described above was over the planned integration of one half of 1 percent of the Centralia Public School students.

CHAPTER

3

ONE METHOD OF
INVESTIGATING
PLANNED INTEGRATION

The planned integration of four schools in Centralia provided
an excellent opportunity for us to study systematically the effects of
integration upon the attitudes and behavior of the people involved,
particularly the students and teachers. A number of questions arose
immediately. What factors facilitate or hinder integration? Could
specific episodes of acceptance and rejection be observed and recorded? What was the general climate of these schools? What was
the relative contribution of administrators, teachers, and students to
the integration process? How could we explore adequately the context
of social interaction in the classroom, playground, lunchroom, or
gymnasium? To what extent was the school influenced by community
groups such as parent-teacher associations or mothers clubs? And
of particular interest was the association, if any existed, between the
integration or assimilation of students and their race and social class.
All these questions were awaiting clear answers. And finally, our
major purpose was to learn about the patterns of social integration.
Integration is assumed to have taken place when the child is assimilated; that is, if he accepts and is accepted by the staff and pupils of
the school. This means that there must be acceptance on the part of
both the old and the new students. The academic achievement of students is beyond the particular concerns of our investigation. We are
focusing on social adjustments.

It became clear during the design stage of our study that the
children participating in the transfer program ought to be compared
with other children to determine whether their experiences were
similar or different. Since the children who had been transferred to
improve racial balance were new to their reassigned schools, the
decision was made to study all children new to a particular school—
that is, children new because they were officially reassigned and
children new because their parents had recently moved to a different

school district. Every child who enters a classroom in a school he has not attended before faces the problem of being integrated into the new group. It could very well be that the problems faced by a black child reassigned to a predominantly white school are no more or less than the problems encountered by a white child or any student new to a particular school. To control for the factor of newness, then, we studied all new students in selected grade levels of the four schools.

Altogether, data were obtained on 656 students in the Centralia public school system (see Table 1). Two-thirds of the students were new to the four schools because their parents had recently moved into the school neighborhood, and one-third were new because they had been deliberately reassigned by the School Board.

Basically, two methods of data collection were used. One method was participant observation. Many studies on the integration of new students into schools have been conducted after the fact; we attempted to study the assimilation process as it was going on. The participant observers were right there as the data unfolded. Four persons, three of whom were enrolled as graduate students in education, sociology, and the social sciences, served as observers. The fourth observer had a master's degree in religion and was a former public school teacher. In fact, two of the observers were former teachers in the Centralia public school system, but they were not assigned to the schools in which they formerly taught. All four of the observers were married and two were mothers. Three were white and one was black; three were female and one was male. An observer was assigned to each school at the beginning of the school year and remained in that school the entire year. About 10 hours a week spent in direct observation and about 10 hours in recording observations. This means that the observer was in the school for about two hours on each of the five school days in a week. Observers were instructed to make observations during varying periods of the day. Each observer was required to learn the names of all new students. At weekly staff meetings all the observers discussed the progress of their observations and the problems they had encountered. The observers sat at student's desks in regular classroom sessions. They interacted with students in the lunchroom and on the playground. They were not regarded as teachers and did not have any authority role in the school.

The administrative staff of the Centralia School District preferred that the observers be called observers. They were introduced to the principals of the schools in which they were to serve by the superintendent of schools at the school district headquarters; the principals, in turn, introduced the observers to the teachers at faculty meetings in the schools. When necessary, the observers explained to the children that they were graduate students making a study of how children get along in school. In general, the observers reported that there was no great enthusiasm over their presence in the schools but that the teachers courteously and coolly accepted the fact that the observers would stay for the entire year.

The observers in the three predominantly white schools had to constantly remind the teachers that they wished to observe all new children and not just the black children transferred from the inner city. Each observer had a large notebook in which his typed observations were filed. Observers were requested to identify children by name, to indicate the race of each child mentioned in the report, to state whether the child was an old or a new member of the student body, and if he was a new member, to indicate whether he had been reassigned by the School Board or was a new neighborhood resident. Observer reports varied in fullness of description and in completeness, but most followed the prescriptions outlined above. These reports provided the data for qualitative analysis of the school integration process.

Toward the end of the school year, the observers were given forms to fill out. In the first part of the form, the observer was asked to rate each new student on degree of assimilation. The question was phrased as follows: "In your opinion, has each child listed been assimilated into the school (that is, has each pupil accepted and been accepted by the staff and pupils of this school) so that he acts as a part of it?" The observer could check one of the following ratings: A = well assimilated; B = fairly well assimilated; C = moderately assimilated; D = poorly assimilated. The second part of the form requested the observer to explain the rating he had given in Part I by indicating whether or not the child had personality, learning, or social interaction problems. Specific categories listed as personality problems were: shy, easily hurt, bully, disruptive, demanding, disturbed. Categories listed as learning problems, were: slow, undisciplined, apathetic, defeated, poor background. Listed as social interaction problems were: does not get along with other pupils or teachers, always late, problem family, bad friends, unkempt. The observer could also indicate "no problem" under the personality, learning, and social interaction sections, and under each of these sections a space was left for write-in problems. Because the specific problem categories were so clumsy, no attempt was made to present a detailed analysis of that material. However, the rest of the data supplied on these forms, especially the assimilation ratings in the first part, were statistically analyzed.

Data-gathering schedules were administered not only to the participant observers but also to the teachers and to the students themselves. Assuming that the participant observers viewed the student's assimilation from a limited perspective, we sought another perspective, namely that of the teacher. We asked the homeroom teacher to fill out one of these assimilation rating forms for each new student. A senior member of the research staff visited the two junior high schools to collect data from the teachers. The assimilation rating form was explained in a faculty meeting, and homeroom teachers were encouraged to rate students before the meeting was over. In this way a good return was obtained on teacher ratings of students. These faculty ratings of students were obtained toward the close of the year.

Finally, as the school year was about to end, students were asked to indicate how they felt about other students and how they thought others felt about them. Elementary school children were given the Colvin Picture Test. First-grade students were excluded. In row C of the test the student was asked to rate himself on a continuum from one to ten with regard to how much other students in his class liked him. The specific instructions a research assistant gave the children during the test were as follows: "Look at the drawing at the top of the page. Make believe that they are pictures of some of the children in your class. The first child, number one on the numbers below, is the best liked boy or girl in the class. The least liked is number ten. I want you to decide about where you belong in the line and put a circle around the right number. If you think you are the best liked person in the class, put a circle around number one. If you are near the best liked, you might circle two or three. If you are near the middle you might circle four, five, or six. The least liked you are, the higher the number you should circle on the third row of numbers. If you think you're near the least liked but not quite, you might circle number nine. If you are the least liked of all the children circle number ten."

The junior high school students were given an opinion test constructed by Robert H. Hardt. The test consisted of 102 questions; we used only one of the questions to get some indication of how some students felt toward other students. Question 19 of the Hardt Student Opinion Test asked, "How many of the kids in your school would you say are the kinds of kids you like? The answers could be (1) almost all, (2) most, (3) about half, (4) a few, (5) almost none. The Colvin Picture Test and the Hardt Student Opinion Test obviously do not ask the same kinds of questions. While the Colvin Test got the youngster to speculate about how well he was liked, the Hardt Test asked the youngster to indicate how well he liked others. It would seem, however, that believing one is thought well of by others and thinking well of others oneself are both related to the process of assimilation. So these items were used as a way of assessing how students viewed their assimilation. Students' views were compared with the views of teachers and observers.

An original plan was to combine the ratings of the observer, teacher, and student, but preliminary analysis revealed discrepancies among the three ratings. Rather than attribute these discrepancies to errors in the perception of one or more of the raters, we thought it probable that the discrepancies simply represented real differences in the ways that students, teachers, and observers viewed the same behavior. So the analysis will be a three-way view of assimilation.

The four-point scale that observers and teachers filled out was reduced for analytical purposes to a three-point scale: the A and B ratings were combined as a single rating of "well assimilated," and the C and D categories of "moderately assimilated" and "poorly assimilated" remained as they were on the original scale. To correspond with this new three-point scale, a response of 1, 2, 3, or 4 on the Colvin Test were considered to be an indication that the student was well assimilated; a response of 5, 6, or 7 indicated that he was moderately assimilated; and a response of 8, 9, or 10 that he was poorly assimilated. On the Hardt Test, answers 1 or 2 ("almost all" and "most") were considered to be an indication that the student was well assimilated, answer 3 ("about half") indicated that he was moderately assimilated, and answers 4 or 5 ("a few" and "almost none") indicated that he was poorly assimilated. By compressing the observer ratings, the teacher ratings, and the student ratings into a similar scale, the data were of course somewhat distorted, but this technique did permit a comparative analysis, a three-way view of the extent of integration or assimilation of all students new to four Centralia public schools.

In the next two chapters we will analyze in detail the four school settings within which the cautious step towards integration took place.

CHAPTER

4

INTEGRATION
COMES TO TWO
ELEMENTARY SCHOOLS

The Centralia School Board's proposal to reassign black young-sters to the Simpson Elementary School and Highland School to de-liberately improve racial balance presents a most interesting situation that is being repeated throughout the country. Our researchers, sta-tioned in the two schools, were able to give us on-the-scene reports of the initial reaction of teachers, students, and principals.

At this point, a detailed description of our somewhat complicated analysis and methodology would interfere with the feeling we want the reader to have of being at home in the four schools. So for the most part we are postponing the more technical approach until the final two chapters of the book.

We were able to compare the pattern of assimilation in two schools that are relatively similar in the socioeconomic status level of neighborhoods surrounding them but that have different orientations to education. The Simpson School has a reputation for being a high-achieving school. While the Highland School has a good academic rating, it is better known in the community as the school for physically handicapped children, although nonhandicapped children also attend it and are enrolled in the same classes as handicapped children. Thus one school had been oriented toward the intellectually gifted while the other had been oriented toward the physically handicapped. Our analysis will help to determine if these two different orientations made a difference in the way new black children were received.

About 18 percent of the Highland students were black, and from 6 to 7 percent of the Simpson students were black. These two schools, then, present an opportunity to explore whether or not the number of blacks in attendance at a school makes a difference in the progress of integration. It has been asserted in the past that the larger the proportion of blacks involved, the more difficult the integration process.

Highland Elementary School became a host or receiving school for black and white students who had formerly attended Bridges and Denison schools. The children who were transferred from these two schools were, by and large, from a lower socioeconomic stratum than most of the children already at Highland. This new enrollment brought the total number of black students to nearly 18 percent of the 530-member student population.

When the plan for desegregation was announced, the principal stated that "it is good and it is healthy. There has been too much parochialism in Centralia, with people living in certain districts and attending certain schools." He was pleased that the Board of Education had at last become committed to a policy of considering racial balance where it had previously ignored the question of integration. He believed that the official action taken by the Board removed the feeling of confusion and of things being "left up in the air."

Highland had a higher academic rating than Bridges and Denison; the principal, therefore, was concerned about the reassigned students. Primarily, he was anxious _for_ rather than _about_ the incoming children; he said:

> I wanted to make sure that the teachers would ac-
> commodate the new youngsters at their pace in school,
> for I thought it might be difficult for them to be placed
> in a new school. But as far as the acceptance of them
> as being black, I was not concerned at all, since Highland
> has had black pupils before without any problems of dis-
> crimination. In other words, I was concerned for them
> as new students and not as black or white, rich or poor.

The principal hoped, too, that the teachers at Highland would be patient and understanding, for the students were, as he expressed it, "victim-ized by an uprooting complex of events." He further stated that the higher socioeconomic level of most children in the existing Highland student body was reflected in their home backgrounds and in their interest in school and their desire to achieve.

Although principals are often subjected to a variety of cross-pressures from parents and teachers, the principal at Highland seemed to have escaped much of the usual ping-pong. According to him, his problems lay with the parents of the incoming black children:

> I did have quite a number of black parents call me. They
> asked me to help them not have their kids come to High-
> land because they lived nearer their old schools and
> seemed to be happy in them. These parents were upset
> about their children being transferred, they didn't want

it, and they wanted me to know it. I pointed out to them that the problem was one of overcrowding at Denison and Bridges and, in view of the fact that Highland had more room, that obviously the children had to be moved and the boundary lines of the school area expanded. I did not receive any distressed calls from white parents. In fact, they didn't call me at all, either before or after the arrival of the new children.

The PTA was, in his opinion, inadequately informed of the Board's plan. Initially, there was a feeling of confusion among its members, and they seemed to be wondering, "Where are we going, what exactly is the policy?" The Board of Education scheduled a meeting in which the Superintendent of City Schools spoke to the Highland PTA. The general tone of the questions put forth by the parents indicated a fear that their children might receive an inferior education as a result of a "slowing down process in classwork to accommodate 'slow learners.'" The speaker said that he thought the quality of education would not be altered at Highland. If any individual qualms did in fact exist among the white parents after this meeting, the principal was not made aware of them. In his words, "These parents bought the plan one hundred percent."

Most members of the teaching staff were not apprehensive about the arrival of the former Bridges and Denison students. The placement of a research observer in Highland whose responsibility it was to report on the development of the integration process was a cause of annoyance for only a few faculty members. According to the observer, these were the teachers who believed that the presence of an outsider disrupted the classroom.

The principal held another meeting prior to the entrance of the students in September. At this session, the teachers heard a school consultant speak on the things to work for in the development of the integration process, reactions to old and new students, exclusion and inclusion in classroom and extracurricular activities, and self-concepts of the former Denison and Bridges students. This consultant was working at that time in one of the predominantly black inner-city junior high schools.

At the beginning of the school year, the teachers were not particularly upset, angry, anxious, or unhappy about the incoming youngsters. According to the principal, teachers felt that in spite of the potentiality for problems, integration in the classroom would be relatively problem-free because of the low teacher-pupil ratio. For the most part, Highland's teachers were experienced, and some of the former Bridges faculty members had been absorbed into the Highland School System. These factors may have accounted for the apparent lack of anxiety in confronting the new situation.

Some teachers tended to equate the position of the new black students with that of the physically handicapped children in Highland. One staff member, for example, was heard to say the following:

> Teachers are experienced here in teaching the handi-
> capped children and this new situation is not anything
> different from our past work. The teachers have always
> stressed individual attention. We had been told in June
> 1964 that the children were coming, but it is within our
> stride and has not presented any problems.

In general, there was a common attitude among the teachers of "taking things as they come."

The average class at Highland was composed of about 18 pupils, and the former Bridges and Denison students were distributed among the classrooms of all six grades. The distribution was uneven, however. In one class of third graders, for example, there were 8 new black children; in another, the majority of new students were white and only 2 were black.

In the first few weeks of classes, it was evident that some teachers ignored or felt uneasy about the black children from Denison and Bridges. The observer noted the following incident:

> In this second-grade class, reading books were being
> passed out. The teacher gave instructions to "take your
> dark crayon and underline the correct answer." Finally,
> after two questions from the children concerning the
> color of the dark crayon, Miss Z said, "the black crayon,"
> hesitating before the word "black." While the class of
> 20 students was completing the work, the teacher had "a
> reading group" as she called it, which was composed of
> one blonde haired white girl, Judy, who was a neighbor-
> hood student. She warned the class to be quiet, that this
> was "Judy's time." Antoinette's hand [Antoinette was a
> new black student from Denison] was ignored four times
> until finally she recognized her with a very stern "what?"
> The teacher then changed to a softer tone to address
> Judy about the reading lesson. Judy appears to be a nor-
> mal reader and was working on appropriate and average
> work for second grade.

In a first-grade class, the teacher chose to tell this story to her students:

> The story was about Harry, a white dog, who got dirty
> from playing in the street. "Have you ever got dirty

from playing in the street?" No one answered. "Well, Harry got black. In fact, he was so black and dirty that no one recognized him. The neighbors saw this dog doing tricks. These tricks were the same as Harry did—but Harry was white and this dog was black. Finally, Harry went into some loose dirt and started to dig. He dug up a brush, a scrub brush. When father, brother, and sister saw him, he was going into the house with the scrub brush in his mouth. Where do you suppose he was going?" Again, no answer. "He went right upstairs to the bathroom and got into the bathtub and here is where the father and the children found him. Father told the children to take the brush and scrub him. The children called their father to 'hurry, come and look!' Harry was the clean, beautiful white dog again."

The observer said that throughout the story Louis, a recently trans-ferred black youngster from Bridges, kept turning around in his seat to sneak a smile at her. The observer is black. There were two other new black children formerly from Bridges in this class.

In still another classroom, the observer noticed that only the new black students were ignored. Some of these students reacted by seeking ways to demand attention:

It was recess time in this class and Bryan, a new black student, had not been chosen by the teacher during the "Dog and Bone" game. After a while, he took a spectro-scope from the desk opposite his, proceeded to tear off the bottom, and let the glass prism lens fall to the floor and break. Mrs. Y said that it had been ruined and no one would be able to look into it any more as the prisms were what made it work. She told him to put it in the waste-basket. His next move was to the bulletin board to look over the gold-starred papers exhibited there. He turned up his nose and returned to his seat where he reached across to another desk, got a magic slate, and began to write upon it.

The nature of student-teacher interaction was satisfactory in most classes. Most of the teachers were quick to incorporate the former Denison and Bridges students into class work and make them feel comfortable at Highland:

In this sixth-grade class, the students are working on Social Studies. Erwin, who is a white neighborhood

28

student who had attended Highland since the first grade, shoved his desk over to meet David's. David is a new student. He is black and he used to attend Denison. They sat together the whole period, at times laughing, at times working, and at times answering questions. The teacher showed no objection to this casual arrangement. He called on David often, prodding him when he gave a half-answer with, "I know you can tell me more, David," or "Yes, you have the right idea." After a while, the teacher announced that "All of you have been such good workers that I am going to let you see a few innings of the World Series game."

Early in the year the observer noted a similar atmosphere in a different class and a similar attitude on the part of the teacher toward the new students:

In this second-grade classroom the seating arrangement is interspersed with black and white children, old and new. There are three rows, with three blacks and two whites in the first row, three whites and two blacks in the second row, and two whites and three blacks in the third row. Bob, a new black student from Bridges, answered the teacher's questions more frequently than any other student. It was apparent that the new black students in general are the most active participants in the class and are encouraged by the teacher: "You did so well on the last question, Bob, do you want to try again?" The white neighborhood students who attended Highland last year do not respond as well. They seem to be more passive.

For the most part, the new students were not isolated from the other youngsters in the classroom. There was little differential treatment by the faculty, not only in terms of separation but also, and especially, in terms of discipline. The former Denison and Bridges children were not singled out if disruptive behavior occurred. Instead, the observer remarked, "If any acting out took place in the classroom which either was initiated by or participated in by the new children, the usual response of the teacher was a verbal 'it's-time-to-settle down' response." There seemed to be no assumption on the part of the faculty that new students would be disruptive.

There was, however, one particular fifth-grade class in which the new children were separated from the old students through seating arrangements and were in fact cut off from responding in class. The teacher's physical and social separation of the children seemed to reflect her attitude toward their "newness" to Highland and not toward their ability or race. The observer described the class:

> There are many children in this class, especially the new students, both black and white, who do not receive attention. They are never called upon by the teacher and are never chosen to answer when their hands are raised. As a general rule, the teacher-pupil interaction in this room centers in the extreme front section of the room where the old established students sit.

Among the classes, some transferees, both black and white, had to be placed in special reading classes which met several times a week. These children were not set apart from their classmates in their own rooms, but they had to leave classes to go to the reading sessions. When these youngsters returned from remedial reading classes to their own classrooms, they were sometimes helped individually, and sometimes at great length, in the regular classroom setting. This special attention could have caused the reassigned children to feel different, but apparently it did not.

> Throughout the work in class, Jim, a new black student formerly from Bridges, showed discouragement. The teacher had to read each item for him. She had him try to read the sentences, but there were many words beyond his repertoire. Even though they occurred again and again in the lesson, he did not recognize them from sentence to sentence. This student was severely handicapped in reading skills but Miss X was patient and devoted the majority of her supervisory time to him. She was not discouraged, but he was. Yet, he did not give up. He would raise his hand and try to answer the question put forth. At the end of the lesson, he began to recognize words more easily and the teacher felt that some progress had been made.

The observer recorded another example of a child, an out-of-state transfer student, who lacked adequate reading skills:

> This third grade is composed of 16 children: 3 new black girls, 4 new black boys, 1 new white girl. The rest are neighborhood students who have attended Highland for some period of time. One black student, new to the school, is a boy from Savannah, Georgia, and was pointed out to me in a whisper by the teacher as having

30

been placed in fourth grade upon arrival but without having records or documentation. His fourth-grade teacher had sent him back to third grade stating that he was not prepared in verbal or in reading skills nor had the foundation necessary for fourth grade. Miss X said, however, that he, like the rest of the students in her class, had an I.Q. above 110.

Some of the former Bridges and Denison students were troubled by a deficiency in verbal expression, although it was clear that they had no problem in comprehending the material presented in class. The following observation depicts the way in which one child began to manipulate conceptual work in her class:

This is a fourth-grade class. The story was "The Secret Cave." Mrs. W asked, "What do you think was the reason for Jeff's fear after the flashlight went out?" Clara, a new black student from Denison, volunteered and answered, "He was afraid that he would slip on glass which was on the floor and bump into it around in the cave." Bonnie, a white neighborhood student who has been at Highland for several years, expanded this comment by saying, "He could be injured on rock formation or could wander afar or into an underground lake or water system." After this clarification of the composition of caves, Clara volunteered again to discuss the dark rocky interior in response to another item, this time using the words Bonnie had used. I could not help thinking that her background had not included caves either in real or vicarious experience but Clara readily learned, altered her thoughts and descriptions, and relayed back to the group in a more meaningful way.

Throughout the year at Highland, the observer recalled only one class in which one of the new students was considered a "behavior problem." Furthermore, the friends with whom he disturbed the class were neighborhood youngsters who, according to the teacher, "had always caused trouble."

In Mrs. W's class there are 3 definite behavior problems: David, a white neighborhood student, and Ronnie, a white neighborhood student, both of them have been students at Highland for a few years, and Bruce, a new black student from Denison. David and Bruce annoy their neighbors by talking to them and getting out of their seats to bother

31

them. When the other children ignore them, they sit
and talk with each other. Ronnie sits in the back of the
room by himself and does what he wants to do—which
includes talking aloud, banging on his desk, and drum-
ming with his pencil. All three boys are classed as above
average in intelligence, but each requires more attention
than the most severely physically handicapped child in
the room.

The observer noted that the relation between the former Denison
and Bridges children and the neighborhood students were friendly
outside as well as inside the classroom. The children played well
together. In the playground and lunchroom the children separated
into groups on the basis of sex; only in the beginning of the year did
they separate on the basis of race.

It was the first day of school in September. Two teachers
were on playground duty and talked together intently,
letting the children play at will. The children were first
and second graders out for noon recess. In looking over
the playground, I noticed 60 children broken up into four
distinct groups: black boys, white boys, black girls,
white girls. The black boys were playing tag, the white
boys were standing around bicycles, white girls were
playing a circle game, and black girls came over to talk
with me. They told me how much they liked Highland. I
could not tell which students were new and which were
not.

A more common scene is described in the following observations:

As the children were getting into line for lunch, a black
girl new to Highland this year left hand-in-hand for
lunch with a white girl from Bridges who is also new.
As I followed the children into the cafeteria, I saw two
new black girls sitting with three white girls who are
also area students. They were sitting at the first
table and were all laughing. As I got closer, I could
hear them asking each other riddles.

The majority of the former Denison and Bridges students found
themselves involved both socially and academically in Highland School
by the end of the first semester of the year. Because of the freedom
in the school and the pervading attitude of acceptance exhibited by the
principal and (with a few exceptions) the staff, the transfer students

responded to their new setting enthusiastically. Most important was the fact that the uprooted youngsters of September became the solidly grounded youngsters of June. A typical example of the new students' perceptions of Highland may be seen in the remarks of a new black girl in the fourth grade:

I like school now. Here, everybody is nice to you. The teachers are nice and so are the kids. The stories in class are better. The teachers aren't mean here. In our school, they used to beat us if we did something wrong. They help us here and they're friendly.

Many reactions from the staff reflected the same enthusiasm:

Third grade teacher:

I have a new black boy in class. I am proud of the way he works. He has made an excellent adjustment. In a few weeks, he'll be taking part in the Christmas play that the students put on.

Sixth grade teacher:

She [a new black student] is a new student and holding her own too, doing all right. She gets along well with the other children. They love her.

Second grade teacher:

Last year, he [a new black student formerly from Bridges] hated school and would not work. F's and D's were the bulk of his grades. Now that he's at Highland, as I was telling his mother, he is as different this year from last as night is to day. He's not an excellent student, but he is an average one and does like school. His mother wanted to know what I had done to change his effort and attitude. She said he likes me too and at home, even, he's a different boy. Well, last year he was in a large second grade and this year it's better for him. I can give him individual attention and his response has been good.

Fifth grade teacher:

The new kids have certainly moved into the school well and have become a part of it. But I wish their parents

would do the same. Not one of the parents of the new
kids, black or white, came to Open House. They [Board
of Education] should have bused every one of those
students years ago.

Seven months after the arrival of the new students, the observer
noted their achievement and assimilation:

These children have come a long way since last September. They now appear capable, poised, and involved
in classroom situations. Perhaps the most important
thing, however, is the fact that they are well accepted by
their classmates. It is difficult now to think of them as
"new students."

In conclusion, it can be said that integration at Highland displayed the markings of success. Recognizing the urgency of desegregation, Highland's principal not only accepted the change but acted as
the primary agent in bringing about a cooperative spirit. Together,
he and a majority of the faculty established a climate for the former
Denison and Bridges youngsters that was responsive to their needs.
They made an unfamiliar school familiar. Most of the new children
felt comfortable at Highland after a relatively short period of time.
Some incidents during the year, however, served to create
problems in the youngsters' adjustment to the school. A few teachers
resented the change that had been thrust on Highland and seemed to
be unwilling to take the extraordinary steps in their classrooms that
would lead to satisfactory relationships between the former Denison
and Bridges children and the "old timers." Thus in a few classes
the new black children were ignored and isolated. But in most instances the adjustment of the school to the new students was favorable,
and so was that of the students to their new school.
The second elementary school we examined was the Simpson
School. The School Board's decision was made public in May, and
Simpson had its first experience in planned integration the following
fall. It was announced then that Simpson would be the receiving school
for 50 to 60 students from Corliss Elementary School, located in the
inner-city area of Centralia. The parents of the Corliss children had
agreed to this transfer.
Corliss does not have a high academic rating in comparison
to Simpson. The majority of its students are black and most of the
students transferred were black. With this deliberate shift, the proportion of black students at Simpson changed from less than 2 percent
to about 7 percent. The transferred students were distributed among
15 classrooms of the first, second, and third grades with a maximum
of 7 in each class. The average class size was 25.

Once the details of the Board's plan were made public, many white parents ceased to be fearful. Others, however, were still not satisfied with this plan to achieve a better racial balance at Simpson.

The Board of Education scheduled one meeting at the school to answer the questions of parents. This meeting was so filled with bitterness and controversy that it merely served to solidify existing divisions within the PTA. After the meeting, the group opposing the plan grew larger and more articulate. Several members of the faction against the busing of inner-city children to Simpson were business and professional people who could present their views forcefully and convincingly. While some were against busing because it violated the "neighborhood school" concept, others opposed it on racial and class grounds. This opposition group has since become a very strong voice in the Parent-Teachers Association at Simpson.

Generally, there seemed to be two prevailing concerns. The Simpson School neighborhood parents feared that their children would receive an inferior education in a diversified student body. Teachers were concerned that the academic reputation of the school would be lowered. These concerns were seemingly based on similar assumptions that the Corliss children would present behavioral problems, have low I.Q. scores, and come from "bad families."

Simpson was proud of its few international students (some of whom were nonwhites) and of its highly respected academic reputation. Blacks who could meet the high academic expectations had been readily accepted in the past. With regard to the transferees from Corliss, however, many of the teachers were apprehensive about their ability to cope with the new students' reputed behavior and academic problems.

Since this was the first planned attempt to alleviate racial imbalance in Centralia, the central administrative staff was in constant contact with the principal and teachers, and a research observer was stationed in the school. This constant surveillance was annoying. The staff's dissatisfaction was often reflected by a lack of security. For example, one teacher questioned the observer in the following manner:

> I don't know what you're doing here. We don't need to be observed. These are just children, treated just the same. This school has always been a little United Nations with Japanese, Korean, Indian, Mexican, all sorts of children coming here. We had three Spanish-speaking children here last year, and they always segregated themselves on the playground; why aren't you studying them? We know how to handle all these different children. Why aren't you studying them

[blacks] in schools where there are more of them? . . .
Who are they trying to kid? I know why you're here.
We teachers all know. And none of us likes being
observed. We are all experienced teachers in the primary grades, more so than you.

One teacher reported that she found the Corliss children "un-
nerving." Anticipating the problems of the coming school year, she
said that "having all these extra children means that the lunchroom,
which used to be a quiet place where children could relax and talk,
will be bedlam." She said that with "all the running on the playground,
teachers are going to have to do double duty and won't like it."
There seemed to be two prevailing attitudes among teachers
concerning the transfer of students from Corliss. According to the
observer, "The young teachers didn't care and the older and more
experienced teachers were panicked."
A teacher typifying the latter category stated that she was further
behind this year than she had ever been during any of her nine years
in Simpson, and that it was because of the Corliss children. This
teacher added, "Anyone who pretends that she has managed to maintain
Simpson standards with these children around is not being honest."
Many of the teachers seemed ultrasensitive to any behavior on
the part of the Corliss children that appeared to differ from the norm.
Many teachers anticipated behavioral problems and therefore quelled
any exuberant behavior by Corliss children before it produced the
anticipated bedlam. As a result, Corliss children were watched
closely. According to the observer, teachers often lectured to the
former Corliss students about appropriate and inappropriate behavior.
For example, the observer who frequently ate with the students noted
the following episode with four blacks eating together in the lunchroom:

Mrs. V had the 11:20-11:45 duty; she began by lecturing
our table, talking about how noisy and messy it had been
the day before. (Actually this table was far quieter than
her own class.)

In a discussion of some of the problems facing the teachers in
the beginning of the school year, one teacher was asked whether she
or the other teachers had talked with the principal, a woman, about
these problems. She responded:

No, because the principal has always been a very
pleasant person who would do whatever was expected
of her. However, this fall she is tense and stern,

36

walking around the halls all the time, too busy for any person. Other years she would drop in any time with no fuss, and the children loved having her. This year she is stern.

Initially, the principal was quite disturbed that there would be a research observer in her school. She felt that this would be disruptive to the teachers and the students. After schedules for the observation of classrooms were established in advance, she became more accepting of the fact that Simpson was being closely observed by researchers as well as by representatives of the Board of Education.

In this early phase of the school year, the special attention given this school took its toll on the principal. However, about the middle of October the observer noted a change in the principal:

> She has begun to relax. In the beginning of the year she did not know these children's older sisters and brothers, she had no contact with the parents. She did not know which were apt to be ring leaders, whom she could call on in a pinch. Now, she is getting to know these pupils as individuals. I noticed in the lunchroom she is no longer the principal with the big stick, but is doing her best to talk these children into good behavior, kidding them, smiling, a bit of cajoling.

The principal and many of the teachers expressed discomfort in their initial relations with the Corliss children. Much of this uneasiness was due to the fact that they had had no contact with the children's parents or older brothers and sisters prior to the transfer.

The observer also noted a tendency to stereotype the black children:

> For many of the teachers who are resisting this transfer, all blacks are automatically considered as being from under-priviledged homes with inadequate backgrounds, and, therefore, intruders to the smooth sailing (S.S.) Simpson.

It should be recalled, however, that some of the black children lived in the Simpson District and came from middle-class families. But when the Corliss children came, the teachers tended to react to old black youngsters as they reacted to the transferred children. Some teachers were able to relate to the new students on an individual basis. Often, particularly in the second half of the school year, teachers would use some of the former Corliss students as "good" behavioral models for the class. For example, a teacher attempting to get the attention of her class said, "April [a black child from Corliss] is the only one in the whole room who is ready." This technique is used very widely by the teachers, who use both Corliss and non-Corliss children as models for the class.

Several very creative and apparently effective techniques we~ used to aid the socialization process of the new students. These techniques were geared to the individual and the particular situational demands. For example, tardiness was widespread in the beginning of the school year, and the following episode is typical of how it was handled in a sensitive and creative manner.

> Elizabeth arrives just after attendance is taken. She is chronically tardy. Elizabeth has a small doll with her. Mrs. T asked her to bring the doll to the front of the room. Mrs. T took the doll and as Elizabeth nervously answers various questions, she kept reaching for the doll. Mrs. T kept it out of the girl's reach. She scolded the doll for making Elizabeth late, even though the child stated that the family got up late. When she returned to her seat, with the doll, she started to comfort it, and Mrs. T asked her to put it into her own desk for a nap.

Many examples of this kind of skill in dealing with the problems of children were observed. A teacher attempted to get total class involvement by asking members to demonstrate, for example, particular aspects of counting. In a second-grade class, a teacher asked one of the former Corliss students to draw six pairs of shoes on the board. This pupil drew six shoes rather than six pairs of shoes. To illustrate, the teacher asked all of the six children in this student's row to place their feet in the aisle for her to count. As a result of this illustration, the student learned the meaning of "pair." Most of these techniques were not used or developed especially for the Corliss students. The Simpson teachers have a reputation for being very creative.

Some of these techniques, such as permitting one student to call on another student for recitation, tended to isolate or exclude the former Corliss student from the main flow of class activity. This hampered new student participation, particularly at the beginning of the year. In the following observation, this method was used and the teacher apparently became aware that the new students were being excluded. To alleviate this, the teacher called on those excluded and "liberally praised" one new student for giving the correct answer.

> Spelling was next. . . . Mrs. T called on a white girl first, and told her to 'invite someone else to do the next

one.' This went on for five answers, involving three
girls and then two boys, all white. Then Mrs. T called
on John (white), Ruth (black) and Yvonne (black). Yvonne
had a particularly difficult question, but she had raised
her hand, and she had all parts of it right, even though
more than half the class had missed one part. She was
somewhat self-satisfied, but in a quiet way; Mrs. T
praised her liberally.

Some teachers divided the students into reading-ability groups.
The majority of the Corliss children were placed in the poorest reading group, which meant that they had to leave the regular class peri-
odically to attend special reading classes. This method of teaching
homogeneous ability groups tended to keep the Corliss students together and also tended to separate them from other students at
Simpson. For example, in one class the observer noted that the best
reading group contained twelve white children and no students from
Corliss. The observer described the composition of one of the poorest
reading groups, consisting of the three former Corliss children and
two white students.

At 10:55, the teacher called five names for the last
reading group, which included all three Corliss children
(in a class), John, a tall blonde boy who sits slightly
apart from the class, directly in front of the teacher's
desk, and Lawrence (who is white, a neighborhood resident). This group reads with the greatest difficulty.

Starting from the first grade, there is a strong emphasis on
reading and the use of words. Since Simpson had received predominantly middle-class students in the past, the majority of the
teachers were accustomed to having children with highly literate
parents and well-stocked personal libraries. The teachers therefore
assumed that the children would be highly verbal and able to read
even in the early grades. The observer noted that in the first grade

there is a tremendous emphasis on words in this room.
Many items are labeled, and the teacher operates on the
assumption that many children read.

For example, in the beginning of the year, one first-grade
teacher said: "A number of our children can read. Would those who
can read already please raise their hands?" About 8 children out of
about 20 raised their hands, and none of these children were from
Corliss. It should be recalled that no class had more than 7 former
Corliss children.

During the second half of the school year, the teachers seemed to have made a greater effort to incorporate the Corliss students into the class routine. In April, the observer noted the following about a teacher at Simpson:

> Today in particular I noticed how many times Mrs. S calls on those students who are new, and particularly those who are apt to be behind. Ali has spent most of his life in Africa, and then the past six months in Finland. Marcus spoke no English when he came three months ago, and the Corliss children are academically wanting by her standards. The glaring thing is the number of times they could give the correct answers.

Again it should be noted that some non-Corliss children have similar deficiency problems that require special attention by the teachers.

The new students became more at ease in their new environment, and by the second half of the year they knew the majority of their classmates. One typical indication of this can be seen in the observer's comment about a game the children were playing.

> She [the teacher] began to explain a game whereby she would appoint one child to sit in the front of the room, with his eyes covered, and back to the students, and tries to guess who is knocking on his chair. The people who come are to disguise their voices. The children were very excited, and this game might have been new to them. Cynthia (a black from Corliss) was the first child in the chair. For the first four children, she was able to guess each time.

The observer indicated on many occasions that the students, both old and new, had no difficulty in playing together. The observer did not report any terms, such as "bused kids" or "those black kids," used by the neighborhood residents to distinguish themselves from the Corliss children. There was frequent opportunity for free interaction between the old and new students. The playground offered what was probably the best opportunity. Several teachers very candidly stated that they were amazed at the extent of the interaction between these two groups. One teacher relates the following incident as a sample of the extent to which old students chose to play with new ones.

> Last Friday, the children were to bring in kites, but only five did. . . . So she divided the class in five teams,

and they were to take turns. Yvonne (a black from Corliss) was in a group with four neighborhood white girls, including Karen. When it was Yvonne's turn, the kite really took off, and soared far above the other four. Yvonne got a look of pure ecstacy on her face as she "entered another world," and the two girls in her group who were still to have turns gave them up so she could continue to fly it. In the afternoon, this teacher supplied them with 12 kites, so each had to be shared by only two pupils. The first person . . . to choose a partner was Karen, and she chose Yvonne. Since that time, they have been very close. Karen is just about the top student in the room.

It should be noted that this free interaction did not always occur. In the early part of the year, the observer noted a great deal of separation by race.

My impression was that the playground was the most segregated spot I had seen. There were clusters of girls, all black, in many spots, and most of the groups of boys playing were with predominantly black or predominantly white. There was not a sharp cleavage at all times, and groups would form, dissolve and reform with a changing racial composition, but the impression was still that of some form of subtle differentiation. At times this would become almost overt. Once a group of four black girls, holding hands, started to approach the spot where I was sitting with four or five white girls and one white boy. As they approached, one of the girls swooped up a second and called towards the four approaching blacks, "You cannot touch me" as the two ran off. This seemed to put the black quartet off, in spite of my friendly smile.

In the latter half of the year, the observer reported in every playground observation that there were no groupings or interactions based solely on race. In one observation the observer stated: "From what I could tell, pursuit was the only game. It took many forms, often mixing grades and definitely mixing races." On another occasion, the following was reported: "The entire playground was mixed by grades and races. There are no evidences of cliques." Increasingly, the observer began to describe the following as typical behavior:

Susan [a white neighborhood resident], the redhead from Missouri, had her arm around Dora (a black transfer

41

from Corliss], and she introduced her as her friend.
On my other side, Michelle [a white neighborhood resi-
dent] and Mary [a black from Corliss] were holding hands,
and vying for my attention. We walked two thirds across
the playground like this, talking. Once I stood still, they
used me as a sort of base for a tag game. Then one of
them got the idea of Ring around the Rosie because of
the way we were standing.

This pattern of free interaction became increasingly common
for both new and old students. However, the observer did report a
few cases in which this interaction was hampered by the white neighbor-
bood residents. In one case, "A girl in a group of about three white
girls started to hold the hand of another girl next to her. Realizing
she was black, this girl said something I could not catch as she veered
away and joined the circle at another point." In another incident, a
group of white area residents were playing a game and they seemingly
pressured another white girl to play with them instead of with a black
girl from Corliss. The observer explains:

One little first grader [who is a white neighborhood resi-
dent], kept protesting she did not want to play, though
three girls from Mrs. R's class were trying to make
her. She told them she was playing with someone else,
and the someone she was referring to was Annette, a
black girl from Corliss. They had been playing together when they first came up to me.

In the classroom, a few teachers were faced with what they
considered to be very delicate situations in regard to the new students.
Some of these children were chronically absent. The reason for this
and the ramifications it had for the children can be seen in the following example. The observer reports:

This child [Flossie] is out of touch with the progress of
the class. She has missed so many times, she is lost.
Two siblings are in basic classes. Two nurses have
made three home visits and told me the mother claims
there is no money to buy bread so she cannot let Flossie
go to school without lunch.

The effect of chronic absence on her classroom performance,
and the extra time required of the teacher is apparent in the following
observation:

Paper was being passed out. "First and last name on your Paper" was the only verbal direction until Mrs. T showed everyone how to fold their papers in four sections. Flossie, who is left handed, had written FL, and then erased it. From this early point in the lesson on she never again did catch up. She stood, borrowed an eraser from Gail, used it, and returned it to Gail. She wrote her name, but in mixed lowercase and uppercase letters. Mrs. T was walking around checking.

"Oh, Flossie, that's not the way you write your name. Stay in the lines." The teacher erased what Flossie had done up until this point, and the child began again. She wrote Flossie _____ in the lines. The next time the teacher checked on work, Flossie was behind. "Flossie, let me see your paper. Did you fold it right?" She had.

The lesson was spelling, am, all, so, said, then, mother, father. Spelling is brought into the first grade curriculum the last third of the year, and Flossie might not have had much spelling before. The proper way to do it is to write the word in a column all the way down the paper. Flossie, instead of writing am six times, wrote six a's, then six m's. Twice the teacher came and helped Flossie, but she didn't realize the way Flossie was writing. She had publicly reprimanded Nancy for doing her words that way, and though Flossie watched the reprimand, she didn't change her methods. She continued to erase as much as she wrote.

This behavior typifies Flossie's classroom performance throughout much of the school year. For many of the Simpson teachers this type of performance tended to confirm their initial assumptions about the abilities of the Corliss children. With this impetus, there was a tendency in the early part of the year for the teachers to assume that most of these students would perform on the same level as the student in the above example.

As the year progressed, it was found that the majority of the Corliss students did not conform to these assumptions made by some of the teachers. In fact, there were Corliss students formerly giving superior performances. Some teachers did not know how to respond to this unanticipated behavior. The following observation is a typical case in which a teacher was obviously confused, as indicated in her final statement, "I give up." Michael's performance had been discussed prior to this observation, and the teacher stated that he had very low I.Q. and achievement scores. As will become apparent,

Michael's performance did not conform to the achievement expectations indicated by his low scores.

"Open to page 248," was the only direction. Michael began to turn to it, without looking at any other student's book. Then he sat with his head in his left hand, and seemed to be staring at the page. The first group of practice sentences were eight sentences or groups of words, and the children had to read the words, telling whether or not it was a sentence. All but three or four hands went up on every one, and near the end Miss P waited longer and longer before calling on a child each time, hoping for those few to also volunteer. No response out of Michael. Then she said, "Now, we shall do these again. Remember, read it out loud, and then tell me the answer." Michael's hand shot up, and she called on him. He read the sentence, and gave the correct response. His reading was slow of pace, but accurate. She praised him liberally but not overly. The second section, on the next page, involved correcting sentences. The class was on the third one before Michael realized they had turned the pages. He turned it, and in one more sentence caught up. Then he volunteered for the next one, and was called on it. This time he read "that" for "what" in the middle of the sentence, but no one else noticed it and he was not called on it. Again praised. During the rest of the lesson, which lasted 25 minutes, Mike stayed with the class. He was called on two more times, and each time was correct. Then the assignment was to write a certain article which had just been done verbally. I [the observer] left the room as the paper was being passed out. Miss P handed me a note: "I give up." According to a standardized reading test, Michael scored on the first-grade level. This teacher explained later that she was surprised he could keep up with the class at the third grade level.

Thus, many of the Simpson teachers were presented with a conflict. On the one hand, they were led to believe for various reasons that all or most of the new Corliss children could not perform on the Simpson level of achievement. They feared that these children would cause the achievement rating of the school to drop. On the other hand, many of these students performed well in the class and did not present "behavior problems." As a result, many of these teachers were forced to take a second look at their prior assumptions. Some of these teachers, at the end of the year, stated that the year had been a learning experience for them as well as for the new students. They said that these children did not fit one "type" in terms of performance or behavior.

Based on the data presented here and the qualitative analysis, it would appear that the integration process was smoother and less turbulent at the Highland Elementary School than at the Simpson Elementary School. While the Highland School received more black youngsters and had a much higher proportion of them in its student population, the integration experience was less stressful for the teachers and apparently for the parents of that school. Much of the ease with which Highland approached this new situation of an enlarged nonwhite population was probably due to the kind of leadership which the principal gave. But part of the absence of anxiety was probably also due to the school's experience with physically handicapped children. As a matter of custom, Highland had accepted all sorts and conditions of children in the past. The orientation the school had developed in dealing with the physically handicapped provided guidelines for assimilating the economically disadvantaged.

These findings mean that the orientation of teachers and administrators, the educational environment, or the school climate are probably more important variables in racial integration than are the ethnic proportion or socioeconomic status level of the new children to be integrated. The findings further suggest that an educational environment or school climate that fosters the integration and assimilation of all sorts and conditions of people, including all races and social classes, must include an orientation among teachers and administrators of accepting persons as they are, as well as an orientation toward achievement and high aspiration. It would appear that the development of both knowledge and compassion are worthy goals for formal education.

45

5

**INTEGRATION
COMES TO TWO
JUNIOR HIGH SCHOOLS**

As we follow the word-by-word accounts of the teachers and students, we get some idea of the unexpected problems that arise as social integration comes to the schools. The schoolrooms described in this study are no doubt typical—almost anyone could find similar schoolrooms in his own area. It is interesting to see what happened at two junior high schools as they cautiously moved toward integration.

Lincoln Junior High School was located in a middle-class neighborhood. There were about four white students to every black student. About 30 new black students, most of them from the inner-city area of Centralia, were reassigned to Lincoln in order to achieve a better racial balance. Monroe Junior High School was located in the inner city. There were about three black children to every white child at Monroe. About 30 new white students were transferred to Monroe to bring about a better racial balance; most of them lived in another inner-city lower socioeconomic status area similar to the one surrounding the Monroe School.

In a qualitative manner, we can indicate the similarities and differences in the way new black children were received at a predominantly white school and in the way new white children were received at a predominantly black school. This also provides us with an opportunity to compare the integration process of students with a social-class background different from and similar to that of the existing student body. It should be borne in mind that the new students were strangers and, to anticipate the findings briefly, that strangers of any race often have similar experiences.

Although the 32 students who were transferred from the inner city to Lincoln Junior High School constituted a small portion of the 237 new children who entered that school in the fall, they were nevertheless significant in terms of the school's reaction to their presence.

Lincoln's principal expressed the following attitude about the new situation in his school:

De facto segregation is when you take a district such as Lincoln which has a black population of 7 percent and create a new district including more disadvantaged, culturally handicapped students and raise the black population to 18 percent.

Commenting upon what should be done, he also stated that

. . . the new black students have to be socialized before they can be educated. It is not right to take kids from one junior high school and drop them into another. We have to be careful not to give the white kids the impression that we let black kids get away with things. The children coming in under the Board's plan cannot cope with the kids already here.

The principal's attitude about the former Monroe students was similar to his reaction toward the research observer's presence at Lincoln. He often expressed suspicion and uneasiness. This is apparent in the observer's account of his first meeting with the principal:

On September 23rd, at 8:00 in the morning, I met the principal in the secretary's office at the school. I was trying to obtain a locker. After he had directed me to see some-one about it, he began a tirade against the City School Board and accused me of spying for the Superintendent of Schools, whom he referred to as "Boss." The Vice-Principal and three teachers were in the office at the time.
    I told the principal that I wasn't a spy for anyone and that all of my observations were strictly confidential. As I started for the door he called me saying that no one scared him because he had the security of the big "R." He then asked me if I knew what the big "R." was and I said I didn't. He explained it stood for retirement. He said he had worked in this "racket" for forty years and neither I nor "Boss" worried him in the least. I left the room.

A few weeks later, the observer again encountered the principal in the faculty room. In this conversation, the principal's original idea of the observer as a spy remained intact:

As I entered the room the principal informed those present that "Boss's spy" was here and everyone should be careful of what he said. I apologized to the principal, saying that I was sorry I hadn't convinced him that I wasn't a spy. He didn't bring the topic up again until Mr. N, a school social worker, came in the room. He greeted Mr. N by saying, "Be careful what you say—or he'll report you to the 'Boss."

Another incident occurred in which the observer noticed the principal's stereotyped opinions of blacks. The principal revealed his feelings in a conversation with the observer, the school nurse, the coach, and another teacher in the faculty room:

As I sat down to have a cup of coffee with the people assembled in the room, the principal began to speak. I realized that he was addressing me. He told me that they had just admitted a "Wonder Boy" to the school. He was a black boy who had been ordained as a minister when he was three years old. The principal said he thought the boy would earn a lot of money because "they" make good preachers and "a lot of people will pay good money to have one of them."

The reactions of the Lincoln parents, according to the principal, were not hostile when they were informed about the Board's plan. In his words, "They showed much less resistance than did parents in other districts, such as the Simpson School District. Lincoln received only two phone calls from the parents concerning this matter of racial balance. I attribute this low resistance to the PTA, which, at Lincoln, is very fair-minded."

When the plan to transfer students from an inner city school was announced, the teachers at Lincoln were apprehensive. They seemed to be afraid that the achievement of the existing students would be hindered by the presence of the former Monroe youngsters. One teacher asked the observer, "What do you do to get these transfer kids to take on responsibility like the other students?" Early in the year, the former Monroe students were branded by many of the teachers as "irresponsible," "troublemakers," "slow learners," "potential failures." These feelings were apparent to the observer both in and out of the classroom:

I observed in Mrs. W's homeroom today. Before the class started she told me that I didn't have to observe in her homeroom if I didn't want to because there were no problems in the class. She did, however, feel that I should

come to her second period class because there were "You
know, the transfers," in that particular class. I explained
to Mrs. W that I was at Lincoln to look at all of the students in general and at the new students, black and white,
in particular.

Another instance was recorded in which a member of Lincoln
staff, the librarian, displayed a negative opinion of the youngsters
who had transferred from Monroe to Lincoln:

> I arrived at Lincoln School at 12:50. The classes had
> begun for the fifth period. I went to the library on the
> second floor. As I was going into the room, Mrs. O, the
> librarian, came up behind me and I opened the door for
> her to go in. We were the only people in the library. Mrs.
> O explained that this year she very seldom left the li-
> brary. "Last year if I had to leave to do something I
> knew that the students would put their passes in the box
> and there would be no trouble. With the students we have
> this year I don't dare leave this room." I said, "Why, has
> there been any kind of trouble?" Mrs. O said, "No, but
> that's because I don't go anyplace where I can't see the
> door. Whenever anyone comes in, I get back before any
> trouble can start."

One seventh-grade teacher was engaged in a "case study" approach that was limited to only the new black transfer students. This
teacher, in giving special attention to the youngsters from Monroe,
distinguished the black transferees from old students at Lincoln by
labeling the former "potential failures." The observer remarked that
this seventh-grade teacher, who looked upon the new black students
as "potential failures," singled out these youngsters in the classroom
by administering special tests to them while the rest of the class
worked on classroom material. Thus, in some classrooms, the
transferees were made to feel "different" at Lincoln.

Particularly at the start of the year, the observer noticed racial
groupings and other signs that seemed to show that the former Monroe
youngsters were isolated from the ongoing processes of life at
Lincoln:

> This is the first week of school for the fall session. The
> bell rang for the end of the first period and the students
> came out of the classrooms and filled the hall with noise
> and confusion. Teachers took up their posts as traffic
> directors in the centers of the halls.

49

I decided to go upstairs to the boy's gym class. The boys were standing in a line against the western wall of the gym. There were 23 boys in this class. Six of the boys were black and the rest were white. Although the boys were supposed to be lined up according to height, they had divided themselves into racial groups. Five black boys who did not have their uniforms with them stood together and three white boys who were without theirs were standing on another side of the room. . . .

I arrived at Lincoln School at 12:35. The first lunch period was nearly finished. I got in line with the rest of the students who were waiting for the second lunch period to begin. By the time I was ready to sit down I noticed that the cafeteria had filled up already. I also noticed that there seemed to be many tables at which all white or all black children sat. . . .

This is a ninth grade home economics class. There are thirteen girls in the class, and nine of them are black. Four of the white girls are new, and four of the black girls are new at Lincoln. The home economics room is the best furnished, best lighted, and most attractive room in Lincoln.

There was a definite racial difference in grouping. The nine black girls sat along the table on the northern and eastern sides. The four white girls sat at the southern end of the table. Each group interacted only with its seated members. One of the white girls, Tone, tried to show off for her group and Mrs. H, the teacher, made her move her chair to the front of the white group and away from them somewhat. Tone went through a few antics after she was moved, pushing her chair back and forth and making comments to the other white girls. This behavior drew no comments or attention from the black girls. . . .

I went to a ninth grade history class. There are 25 students in the room, including one new white boy and one new black girl, formerly from Monroe. The rest of the class is composed of three black students who live in the area and 20 white students who live in the area.

Michael, the new white child, didn't know any answers and left blanks on his paper. He looked around the room while the other students wrote on their papers. The new black student, Leslie, kept her eyes on her own desk and apparently knew the answers. There was a racial grouping to this class. All four black students sat in the first two rows. All the white students were sitting in the remaining four rows.

Adjustment to Lincoln was difficult for both the new white students and the black youngsters who had previously attended Monroe School. Throughout the year, various teachers complained to the principal that the new children were "defiant" and engaged in "agitating behavior" in their classes. The observer noted that the principal responded to the complaints by stating that he would "get the School Board representative after them" (that is, the new school social worker). Many of the teachers consistently separated the "troublemakers" from the other students:

> There are 20 students in this art class, 10 boys and 10 girls. It is composed of seventh-grade students listed as a "slow" group. Joe, a new white student, got up from his seat and faced the class. He had heard Miss P call for the girls only but he stood up anyhow. She reminded him that he wasn't a girl and Joe sat down with a pleased look on his face. He was sitting at a table which is pulled away from the rest of the class. Miss P usually puts "troublemakers" by themselves at this desk. During the period Joe was constantly badgering the teacher for attention. Miss P has a policy of calling students to her desk to look at their work. Normally she goes by alphabetical order and only speaks to the other students if they are causing trouble or need special help. Joe was the first one called. He went to her desk and an argument ensued about his work. Miss P said he had done a good job, but it was the same thing someone else had done. Joe said, "I did what you told me to do," and Miss P denied that she had said that. He informed her that he would not do another project. He finally left her desk, loudly protesting and claiming he had been wronged. As other students went to confer with the teacher, Joe would interrupt and ask questions. He was seeking attention which he did not receive.

Although both black and white new students were treated differently from the established students in many of the classrooms, the former Monroe children suffered by far the greater injustice. When disciplinary situations arose, the new black students often received unusually "harsh punishment." The observer recorded an incident that reveals the type of action taken by the administration against a new transfer student from Monroe:

51

The bell rang for the start of the third lunch period at
12:11. While I was standing in line outside of the cafeteria I noticed James, a white area student who has regu-
larly attended Lincoln. He is a ninth-grade boy whom I
have seen in gym class several times. He was fooling
around with several other boys and the horseplay was quite
rough. The boys were hitting each other and pushing each
other out of line. Mrs. A, a ninth-grade teacher, walked
past but said nothing to the boys. (All were white.) Mr.
P, who was serving as the hall monitor, did not come up
to do anything to the boys. Miss J, a ninth-grade teacher,
also walked by but did nothing.
    I mention this incident because it was at this same
spot in the lunch line where Larry, a former Monroe student and a black boy, was caught for doing the same thing
as James was doing and it led to his suspension. Yet,
nothing was done to the white area students and in particular to James. James has a reputation for being a trouble-
maker and I have seen him exhibit nothing but disruptive
and malicious behavior in the school.

Some of the new black pupils were so acutely aware of the manner
in which they were treated by various faculty members that they reported their perceptions to the vice-principal. The observer reports
that at one point during the spring semester two of the former Monroe
students, both eighth-graders, went to the vice-principal concerning
their feelings:

The school board representative at Lincoln told me a
seventh-grade teacher was reported to the administration
by two new black boys, Ray and Jerry, for what they considered to be prejudicial treatment in class.
    The boys told the vice-principal, in his presence,
that their teacher made them say "please" for everything
they requested but did not make this demand of the white
students, in the same class. The boys have Miss L for
a study hall and she will not let them go to the library
during this period. The vice-principal listened to the
boys and then suggested that since they only have this
teacher for one period, they should try to overlook her
behavior. One of the boys, Ray, said he didn't feel they
had to overlook her treatment of them since they had her
study hall several times a week. He was insistent that
something be done about the situation. Ray then stated
that he would call up his mother for support, if this was

52

needed to back his position. According to the school board
representative, the boy's mother did arrive at Lincoln the
next day to find out whether her son could be supported in
his claims.

Several times during the school year the Lincoln School Board
representative (the social worker) spoke with the observer about the
problems of the school. The school social worker made this statement:

> I have had a feeling that some of the teachers and others
> here at Lincoln are quite prejudiced. Some people from
> CORE were here to investigate the violation of one of the
> student's rights. I know that several of the kids' civil
> rights have been violated. A new black student in the
> seventh grade, Tom, had refused to say the words, "with
> Liberty and Justice for all" when his class pledged alle-
> giance to the flag. He, instead, said, "with Liberty and
> Justice for Some." This caused some concern with the
> teacher. Tom explained to the teacher that he felt the
> "for all" portion of the pledge is false. He was reported
> to the principal and the CORE officials became involved
> in the incident in support of the boy.

The school board representative's charge of prejudice at Lincoln
was directed in part towards the principal. One issue that came up
at Lincoln involved complaints from some businessmen in the school
area who threatened to close their stores during the time that the
students were coming to and returning from school. It was their
opinion that Lincoln students were stealing items from their places
of business. When the principal heard of the complaints, he said,
"They don't even know if it was someone from Lincoln. It could have
been kids from another school. I don't think it was a Lincoln student,
not even the colored ones." The sentiment invoked in this remark
seemed to fit with the general pattern of response displayed by some
teachers in their attitude towards Lincoln's black students.
Some of the new pupils, both black and white, were unable to
conform to the structure of learning at Lincoln. The reactions of
these youngsters were identical. As the observer reports, they simply
withdrew from the class setting:

> Mrs. Y began this eighth grade science class by giving a
> practice session of questions which would be similar to
> those asked on the test the children were about to take.
> It lasted ten minutes and then Mrs. Y read 25 multiple

53

choice questions to the class. Carl, a black area student, who has been at Lincoln, seemed to have no trouble and answered all the questions. John, a white area student who has also attended Lincoln for several years, puzzled over some questions and left two of them blank. As the last question was being asked by Mrs. Y, a black boy walked into the room, took a seat away from someone, and stared straight ahead with no expression on his face. Mrs. Y went over to him and said, "Take out a piece of paper Alan and I'll give you the questions while the rest of the class is finishing up." Alan said, "I'm not taking a test." "Come on Alan, get some paper." "I told you I'm not taking a test." Mrs. Y finally said, "Alan, if you don't take the test you'll get a zero. Now get some paper out." The rest of the class was watching them. She said, again, "Alan, get a piece of paper." "What did I tell you? I'm not taking the test and that's it." Mrs. Y walked towards her desk, obviously shaken, and said, "Well, I guess it's up to you but don't blame anyone else." Alan sat until the class ended and then left the room ahead of the others. He is a new transfer from Monroe

. . .

I took a seat in the middle of the northern section of this ninth grade classroom. Joel, a new white student, came into the room with Ron, a black student who has been at Lincoln for two years. Mr. D began to take the attendance. A voice came over the loudspeaker and Joel responded to it with a resounding "Hello." The class laughed and Mr. D told Joel to be quiet. Mr. D was quite provoked and Joel continued talking. He was again reprimanded with the threat that if he persisted in this behavior he would have to stay after school. Joel said he didn't care because he had to be there anyhow. Mr. D, voice rising and face flushing, informed Joel that if he kept it up he would stay after school for the entire week. Joel said, "That's up to you. I don't care." The teacher got very excited and asked Joel to leave the room. And said he would be in detention for two weeks. Joel complied and left the room.

It was a common experience for the new students to help one another in class if they were having difficulty in answering the questions posed by the teacher. In such cases, there was a good deal of interaction between the former Monroe students and the new white youngsters. The observer noticed that this kind of mutual-assistance behavior was exhibited particularly during the latter half of the year as a defensive measure against the older, established students:

> This eighth-grade math class has three new black students and three new white students, all girls.
> The class began at 8:40. The first part was devoted to homework. After the papers were handed in, the class started working on new problems and Mrs. H picked different youngsters to go to the board and put the answer up for the class. During this time, none of the new students volunteered to go to the front of the room. They were holding conversations with each other while the students who were not new were giving the answers. Cindy, a new white student, was chosen to go to the board and work. She didn't appear to be too sure of what she was putting down. She turned around and gave a "help me!" look to Deborah, a former Monroe student. Deborah shook her head as if to tell Cindy that her answer was not right. She then held up some fingers and Cindy, nodding, turned around and did the problem again. This time it was completed correctly and Mrs. H chose someone else to take Cindy's place at the blackboard.

In certain classes, the new transfer students acted as informal class leaders and, at times, were able to control the work at hand and manipulate the teacher's direction of it:

> In this ninth-grade business class, the work consists chiefly of Mrs. P reading the correct way of organizing the balance sheet. All of the students, except three, appeared to be involved in the material initially. The three students who were not participating were Elliot, a new white student, Eugene, a black student, who has been attending Lincoln for several years, and Janice, a white student, who also is part of the existing student body. Elliot sat staring off in space or turning around to look out the window. Mrs. P asked him what he was doing and he replied, "nothing." She said, "As long as you are in the room you'll go through the motions." He didn't respond to her or do any work. Mrs. P then asked Eugene if he was "with the class." He said he got lost the day before and hadn't caught up. Janice was talking and laughing continually. The teacher told her to be quiet and stop distracting her neighbors.

Debra and Susan, both black students formerly from Monroe, would ask questions and answer them by calling out "Mrs. P!" before they spoke. They changed the whole tempo of the class, Debra frequently made noises such as clearing her throat to emphasize her responses. She threw her arms up in the air at times. Her answers were always correct. Once, she caught a mistake Mrs. P had made in labeling one account. Debra belabored the point after the teacher admitted her mistake, doing it in such a way that she was congratulated for sensing the error. Debra was in complete control of her gestures and explanations. Mrs. P was moved to remark that Debra would be a good book-keeper because of her attention to detail. Both Debra and Susan, who had answered many questions correctly, were held up as "models" for the class which, in effect, centered around them.

Activities outside the classroom, as in gym period, provided other opportunities for informal leadership. The observer noted an eighth-grade gym class in which a former Monroe student acted as a leader:

Eleven boys were present in this gym class. The only new, and black boy was Ted. He seemed to be relaxed with the other boys. They, in turn, seemed to be attracted to him and he was involved in quite a bit of "chatter" while the activity was taking place. Ted was chosen to head one group of five boys for drills. He lined his boys up and told them how to do the particular drill they were working on. One of the drills called for someone to stand in the center of the circle. A short white boy who lives in the area and has been at Lincoln two years, took his turn in the center of Ted's group. The boys started to throw the ball to each other and over the short boy's head. Ted grabbed the ball and told them to stop. He said, "Bounce it on the floor, give him a chance." When the small boy finally finished and came back to the circle, Ted roughed up the boy's hair. He grinned at Ted and took his place. For the rest of the period, Ted played fairly and unaggressively. He is clearly in command of the group.

A seventh-grade history class, taught by the only black teacher at Lincoln, involved a great deal of "give-and-take" between the teacher and her class. The observer captures the flavor of this particular class in the following report:

There are 25 students in this class, including two new black pupils and seven new white pupils. The room was filled when I walked in. Miss T told the class that the principal and Mr. N would be in the room but they were not to be afraid of them. The students all laughed when she suggested they think of the visitors as "people," for a change. Miss T explained that the students were giving papers on immigrant and minority groups and their contributions to U.S. culture and society. At the end of the presentations, members of the class would ask questions, discuss the relative merits of the papers, and suggest what grade each student who made a presentation should receive. The basis for the grades was a judgment on the voice projection of the student, the material in the paper, and how well the student used his personal opinion and defended what he said. The first paper was given by Thomas, a new black pupil. It was entitled "The Contributions of the Negro." Thomas dealt with Civil Rights, Science, Education, Music, Law, and International Relations. Part of this student's discussion was a detailed description on "how the white man could let the black alone when he is engaging in any endeavor." (I speculated that perhaps Tom would like this philosophy to be effected in Lincoln.) Members of the class, including 5 new white students, discussed and then evaluated Tom's paper, which was given an "A." Many of the white students stated that his presentation was "informative."

During the period, other papers were given on "Jewish Contributions to American Society" and "Irish Contributions to American Culture." Throughout the presentations, Miss T gently led the class and prompted voluntary student evaluations.

In summary, the new students at Lincoln became familiar with the principal's policy ("get tough with them and they'll come around") and the teacher's preaching ("good behavior is good citizenship"). Several of the new students did not become well acquainted with students who had been at Lincoln the previous year. However, many transfer and other new students, both black and white, coped with the system and related to the old students both in and out of the classroom.

Monroe Junior High School, which is predominantly black, became a host school for 52 students transferred from Plymouth School, which was predominantly white. Plymouth, which had had students of both junior high and elementary levels, became an elementary school only. The reassignment was made in connection with the Board of Education's plan to desegregate the city's public schools; however, only 31 of the students transferred to Monroe were white.

The transfer of the new children caused no change in the racial composition of the student population at Monroe.   The ratio of black to white students remained at about 77 to 23.

Plymouth Junior High School, like Monroe, was not considered to have a high academic rating. A majority of the Plymouth students lived in the neighborhood surrounding the school, and this neighborhood, like the Monroe district, was low in socioeconomic status. Many of the children who attended Plymouth came from families of Italian ancestry. In general, the residents of the Plymouth School District, like those of the Monroe School District, have a lower median family income and lower educational level than residents of most other areas in the city.

When the Plymouth parents were told of the Board's plan to transfer their children to Monroe, they were not enthusiastic although they did not vigorously oppose it. Monroe's principal described the situation as he saw it:

> If the Plymouth parents had any real concerns, they were
> never voiced. At the same time, they never said they were
> for integration. Their grievance against the School Board
> for this policy of closing up Plymouth and shifting the stu-
> dents to Monroe lay in the fact that they were upset that
> their children would have to walk farther to school. I did
> talk with some parents on an individual basis, however,
> and found that there was concern on their part in having
> their youngsters go to a school where the majority of stu-
> dents was black. They were afraid that fights would occur
> and their kids would be socially "left out" of activities. I
> told them that Plymouth had too few students (at the junior
> high level) to get a good educational program there, they
> did not have the facilities which junior high schools should
> have as mandated by the state, and there was no lunch facili-
> ty available, so the youngsters could not stay in school all
> day. It was my personal belief that the Plymouth children
> would have been transferred in any case; be it racial bal-
> ance or for the fact that Plymouth could not survive due to
> its lack of necessary equipment.

During the first few weeks of school, the observer noticed that teachers in Monroe constantly issued warnings against "wrong be-havior." The former Plymouth students, like the youngsters who had attended Monroe the previous year, were not exempt from such ad-monishment:

This is a seventh-grade English class. It consists of 15
children—12 blacks, and 2 white boys, formerly from Plymouth, and 1 white girl from outside. The teacher, Miss
W., was reading to the class from a book. The children
reacted appropriately to various parts of the story and
were listening attentively. Charles, one of the Plymouth
boys, sat in the row of seats by the windows between two
other students. As he listened to the story, he walked
his fingers down the desk of the boy in back of him. As
Charles' hand came near the boy, this boy made a play-
ful pass at Charles. Both boys watched the teacher to
guard against getting caught. The story being read was
a mystery story whose moral was that "wrong-doers sow
the seeds of their own destruction due to the fact that they
feel guilt over their crime and therefore slip up in some
way which later betrays them." Miss W commented that
she does not allow any of the children in her class to get
into trouble. She asked the class if any of them had ever
received a "blue ticket." Charles raised his hand. Miss
W said, "Well, I'm sure it was not for some serious
crime. And besides, that is all in the past. That is all
wiped off the record and forgotten. Now you are in my
homeroom and you are not to get into any more trouble.
I know you will have good records while you are with me."
The other Plymouth boy, John, said, "Since he already has
one blue ticket, does that mean that the rest of us can all
get one to get even with him?" "No, indeed," answered
Miss W "Charles received that ticket before he came
into my homeroom. As of right now is what counts."
Miss W then told the class that she expected them to be
at school every day and those days they were not there
she would call to check with their mothers to find out
why. Any child who misbehaved in class would have to
stay after school. She stated that if she discovered one
of "her children" staying after school for another teacher,
they could expect to stay for her too.

In the beginning of the year, the white students from Plymouth
seemed not to participate in the activities of the class. They generally
withdrew:

It is the second week of school. In this ninth-grade class
two white boys, formerly from Plymouth, were sitting together by the windows. Both looked sleepy and were posi-
tioned generously in the seat and across the table. They

were not taking notes, books were piled up on top of each other unopened, and one boy had to struggle to keep his eyes open at all. His feet were widely spaced beneath the table, one straight out in front, one to the side. His head was resting on his books, his head facing the teacher, and one arm was under his head while the other arm lay across the table. The other boy was sitting low in the chair with his head resting against the back of it. Mr. C finally said to them, "All right, you boys, sit up in your chairs." The two black boys sitting closest to them exchanged smiles. Not once did the two Plymouth boys answer questions or in any way relate to what was going on in the room.

While the transfer students were not taking part in academic activities they were mildly disruptive in class. Again, this kind of behavior was exhibited in the early months of school. Since these students did not know many of the Monroe youngsters, they seemed to feel the need to draw attention to themselves in class so as to make the other children and the teacher recognize their existence. The observer recorded the following incident as typical of the former Plymouth students' activity:

This is an eighth-grade social studies class. There are 24 children in the room. Sixteen are boys, four of them white from Plymouth. There are eight girls, one of them white from Plymouth.
 The child who made his presence known most was John, a transfer from Plymouth. His manner was disruptive in that he constantly spoke out without waiting to be called upon and several times got out of his chair and roamed about the room. He and two other white boys sat in a row together. The other two were quiet, not participating in the recitation but aware of what was happening in class. They followed directions from the teacher. The remaining white boy played around with the black boys on either side of him in their row. He moved the desk of the boy in front of him, and that boy turned about and socked the white boy, not hard, and smiling as he did it. The two black boys and the white boy often exchanged remarks and seemed to be on friendly terms with each other.
 The lone white girl in the class sat quietly, did not talk to any of her neighbors, nor did she volunteer during the class work. The last part of the class was occupied by reading aloud from a book dealing with courage. John, the new white student, jumped to his feet, walked to the

front of the room and spoke to the teacher, loudly complaining about not having been chosen to read from the book. Mr. N sent him back to his seat and said he would have an opportunity to do so. When Mr. N called on Jackie next, a black student from Monroe, John again walked up to Mr. N's desk and announced that it was now his turn. Mr. N let Jackie finish reading and then called upon John who read well until the class ended. As this class broke up into various reading groups, I followed one bunch of children into another room where I noticed seven black girls, five black boys and one white student from Plymouth about to take their seats. The white boy was a tall gangling youngster. He and two short little black boys worked together fashioning a noose of the window cord, taking turns trying to hang each other. The objective in this room seemed to be "have as much fun as possible before the teacher arrives!"

Most teachers at Monroe did not ignore the former Plymouth students or separate them from the ongoing process of classroom activity. Some teachers, however, tended to bypass the new transfer students:

There are six boys in this class—four white Plymouth children and two black students who have previously attended Monroe. There are also 15 girls—13 black and 2 white (one from Plymouth). The tables are arranged in a large U shape. The four white boys sat beside three black children at one table, and the two white girls sat together at the other end. They whispered, laughed and in general paid not the slightest attention to the class activities.

One of the white boys was asleep. Another white boy moved to a table by himself and stretched out across two chairs in full length. He looked comfortable, but was not interested in the business at hand. Two black boys in the back of the room were laughing, but stopped when the rest of the class did not respond. The class discussion was on gravity. Mr. B was asking questions and the group inside the U portion of the table was eagerly raising their hands. This group was composed of black girls from Monroe. They seemed interested in the subject and in getting the correct answers. Because of their behavior, Mr. B kept feeding them information and questions very rapidly. Occasionally, they would not get quite the right

answer or not the complete answer and he would take time
to show them why another answer would be better. These
students really knew what was going on and showed it. They
contributed much to the class, were quick and bright, and
were rewarded by the teacher as he constantly challenged
them. The girls expressed themselves clearly and con-
cisely. With this group, there was no need for the teacher
to establish order first and teach second.

Mr. B, who usually does not permit sleeping in class,
was caught up in the excitement of the Monroe students'
response and consequently let the boys from Plymouth
sleep. At the same time, he seemed to forget their presence.

During the course of the year, there was an increasing tendency
on the part of the white students from Plymouth to mix with the black
students at Monroe. In the early weeks and months, the observer noted
that white students tended to group with each other in some classrooms
and in the lunchroom. Towards the end of the first semester of the
school year, the separation of racial groups seemed to disappear as
the students came to know one another. The observer describes this
tendency in the following report of three seventh-grade classes who
were watching a movie in the lunchroom:

Four white girls, three from Plymouth and one from outside, were flanked on each side by a black student. They
were obviously enjoying each other's company and were
quietly talking so as not to attract the attention of the
teachers. At times, they whispered in each other's ears,
and at other times exchanged written notes on the movie.
The white boys were dispersed throughout the room;
among the boys of course; seventh-grade boys do not sit
with seventh-grade girls! No two white boys sat together.
I have noticed since the year began that the boys formerly
from Plymouth are more inclined to mix in with all the
boys, and white girls tend to stay more together. Today,
however, I am not aware of the girls "sticking together."

It was the observer's opinion that as time wore on and the "settling
down" process took hold, the Monroe youngsters showed increased
evidences of acceptance of the new students and, in turn, the transferees became more relaxed and accepting of the old students. Some
of the white students from Plymouth, particularly the girls, were
increasingly included where before they had been excluded.

When the school year began, the "in" group of Monroe students ostracized the new children. In the observer's words, it was as if the old students were saying, "You see, we are friends and we don't know you but we want you to be aware of how close and friendly we all are." The barriers began to break down from day to day as the once strange environment became familiar, and by the end of the year these barriers had disappeared. One example of the kind of exclusion prevalent at the start of school is reported by the observer:

> This is a seventh-grade homeroom. There are 25 children present. The only white girl is Nancy, formerly from outside. She has hair that is never combed, her clothes are not cleaned or pressed, and she looks unkept in comparison to the other children. Nancy tried to get in with some of the black girls from Monroe who are area students. They were "doing bad things" like opening the door, stepping out into the hall, and laughing and talking. They were enjoying every moment of flirting with potential danger! When Nancy attempted to join them in such sinful activity, they cut her dead, turning their backs on her and whispering together to make the exclusion more final. Nancy walked back to her desk. She leaned forward and began to touch the hair of the girl ahead of her. The girl did not like this at all and shook her head impatiently. Finally, Nancy drew her into conversation and the girl did not shut her off unkindly but chatted with her. Nancy wants to be a part of the group, any group. She tried in four different ways in a few minutes to do the things the group did and in the group's way. The Monroe children were not having any part of her. However, There seemed to be no racial overtones in the girls' rejection of Nancy. Rather, she was not "in" and when she tried to copy the "in" behavior she was ludicrous.

There was no overt evidence that the lack of acceptance of any child by any other was based on race. There was no fighting or name-calling either inside or outside the class. If racial feelings did exist they took subtle forms. It was rather that pre-existing friendship patterns were the basis of student groupings at Monroe. Children who had been friends before, either at Monroe or Plymouth, determined who could interact with them, at least in the beginning of the year. The white children from Plymouth, although they might not have known one another in their old school, were drawn together by having come from the same school and by being members of a minority group in a new setting. Furthermore, a majority of the former Plymouth students lived in a different neighborhood from most of the Monroe students and had a long walk home. When the children left school for the day, it was more common to see a white boy with a group of black boys than a white girl with a group of black girls. White girls who were transferred to Monroe seemed to be the most isolated group in the school. Black girls, however, according to the observer, interacted freely with all of the other children—white or black, girls or boys— particularly in the latter half of the year. As the classes progressed, some of the former Plymouth students became more involved in their work and the various learning experiences.

A few of the new transferred students were disruptive and engaged in attention-getting behavior; others were withdrawn, and some were quiet, studious, and attentive:

> This is a ninth grade Spanish class. There are 10 chil-
> dren in the room. Seven are black, three are white. Two
> of the white children are neighborhood students who have
> previously been at Monroe; the other white student is a
> Plymouth transfer. Vertise, a black girl from Monroe,
> answered most of the questions put forth. She had an
> excellent grasp of what was being taught. Running a close
> second were Leo, a black boy from Monroe, and Ethel, a
> black girl who moved to the area from Mississippi. The
> teacher, Miss M, informed me later that Ethel was the
> best student in her class but that all of them were good.
> Dennis, the white boy from Plymouth, was quiet most of
> the period but answered questions when he was called
> upon. He seemed to be totally absorbed in the work, took
> notes during the class and responded to Miss M's ques-
> tions with knowledgeable ease. He did not, however, raise
> his hand nor initiate any participation. Dennis did not
> appear to be shy, but waited for the teacher to provoke a
> response from him. His face reflected delight when he
> answered correctly.

Many of the classes at Monroe are geared to the childrens' various levels of ability, capability, and productivity. There is a special education class for students who cannot keep up with the work handled in regular classes. It is a small class of only four students and is unique not only in terms of the material presented but also in terms of the behavior exhibited in it. The observer related the experiences of this class:

> Mrs. R tailors the work to suit her students' abilities.
> There are two boys and two girls in the class. One of the

boys is a white transfer student from Plymouth. One of the girls is a black area student who moved here this year from Florida. The atmosphere in this class is friendly. The children came in chatting and happy. Mrs. R had them come to her desk one at a time while she checked to see what they had worked on the day before and what their assignment was for the day. Ray, the white Plymouth youngster, is cocky with a smart remark always in readiness. He wears built-up shoes which clicked noisily as he walked around the room. He listened while he was given instructions, nodding his head to indicate he understood. He proceeded to go to his desk where he placed books on the floor, picked them up, put them back down, and generally wasted time. He began to work and a few seconds later spoke out loud to Mrs. R "What am I supposed to be doing with these things?" "What do I do with adjectives and adverbs?" Mrs. R got up and went to his desk. "Is this the page I told you to work on?" "This is what you told me." "Ray, do you know what an adjective is? Define it for me, you had it just yesterday. What does an adjective do?" Ray could not answer but leafed through his book and found it. He then looked away, fingered some pages, and flipped them randomly.

Martha, the black girl from Florida, is quiet. She looks downcast and is withdrawn. Her job was to reduce fractions. Mrs. R had to go to her and help her correct them. Martha did not talk with any other student, nor they with her. Toward the end of the class, Ray took his work up to Mrs. R to be checked. She sent him back to complete it. Ray was unhappy about this, and said, "I'm not going to do it. I don't know how and I'm tired of working on it." Mrs. R replied, "Ray, this assignment is already two days old. You have two zeros already and this will make a third." Ray looked at her and stated, "Oh, I could almost care," and walked over to another part of the room to gaze at something. He did not do his work and spent the rest of the time at his desk sitting with his feet stretched out as he loudly drummed on the desk.

This class, which does not have the status of a basic class, is a study in contrasts. It typifies not merely the defiant or withdrawn behaviors associated with children who have many problems but, moreover, suggests the nature of a conflict that the teacher must confront—the teacher is caught between the attempt to reinforce the lessons of formal grammar and the opportunity to encourage thought and investigation.

Some of the former Plymouth children, even towards the end of the school year, were still on the fringes. They did not relate well with the established children in Monroe, the new school to which they were assigned. Isolated incidents in the classrooms reflected this notion of them as outsiders. The observer frequently remarked, for example, that when the students were allowed to choose their own seats, the transfer pupils would always sit in a front seat, a back seat, at the end of a row, but rarely in the center. It was as if these young-sters were quite literally placed "on the fringes" of the class.

There seems to be little administrative concern about children who are able to fit into the system but are unable to fit in with other students. The life experiences of some of the former Plymouth young-sters differed from those of some of the Monroe students. No school program to bridge these differences was initiated. It was left to the individual pupil to become absorbed in the climate at Monroe.

The observer recalled a guidance class held at the end of the year in which the teacher asked several black students from Monroe how they would like being in a class with mostly white children. Their answers reflected a certain fear of moving into an unknown situation that would be dominated by white students: "It would be okay with a gun." "I'd take my knife with me." "I wouldn't like it but I guess I could get used to it." The teacher asked them why they would need a knife or a gun. "Well, you don't know when they'd gang up on you," came the response.

The Plymouth students did not express this kind of fear. Most of them began to feel comfortable at Monroe by the second semester. One boy who had transferred to Monroe in the fall wrote an essay in the school newspaper, and the opinions he presented seemed to be shared by a large number of other students who were formerly at Plymouth.

I like it here as much as I did at Plymouth. The teachers are understanding and the kids are friendly. The work isn't easy but when you do it it helps you get along with the teachers. The books and other materials are more plentiful than at Plymouth. The principal is nice and I like to take his advice. The vice-principal and counse-lors are fair in solving problems. The rules are a bit tough but I guess you need rules to run a good school.

In spite of the hostile climate of Lincoln or the laissez faire setting at Monroe, the reassigned white and black children began to become a part of their new schools during the latter half of the school year. This indicates that there may be a development process to integration, moving at its own pace once white and black or poor and affluent youngsters are brought together; therefore, any assessment of the success or failure of integration in the schools would need to indicate the time in which the assessment is made. The racially homogeneous groups during the first semester transformed into racially heterogeneous groups the second semester. All this points toward the need for more information on the different phases of the integration process and the conditions under which they are shortened or lengthened.

It is sometimes asserted that the process of racial integration is more difficult when the persons involved are also of different socio-economic status levels. A qualitative analysis indicates that lower-class youth who were transferred to a middle-class school were treated as strangers during the first semester and not admitted to the fellowship of the many different groups in that school. Likewise, the lower-class youth who were transferred to another lower-class school were shut out of the informal groups and they too were treated as strangers. Thus, it would appear that the newness of the students to each other is a more important variable limiting interaction than differences or similarities in their social class. This principle is stated in a tentative way because of the limited class levels available for analysis.

Finally, we see that the reassignment of students to improve racial balance is only the beginning of the integration process, and that probably as much attention needs to be given to preparing the schools as to preparing the children. Neither Lincoln nor Monroe were prepared to foster the assimilation of new children into the existing student population. The school year was basically a trial-and-error experience with some teachers trying harder and others erring greatly. And the children were blamed for the staff's mistakes; they were blamed for being what they were and for coming from where they came; they were blamed for not being like the rest of the children; they were blamed for being new.

6

THE ROLE OF
TEACHER AND PRINCIPAL
IN INTEGRATION IN
THE FOUR SCHOOLS

The attitudes of the principals and teachers of the four schools in our study (Highland, Simpson, Monroe, and Lincoln) are important factors to consider in our approach to social integration problems. In the previous chapters we stressed the students' reactions to integration. In examining the teachers' and principals' reactions, the differences and similarities in the schools again become apparent. It will be important to seek explanations of the kinds of adjustments made and to identify the factors that facilitate or interfere with the process of integration.

Two of the schools, Simpson and Lincoln, displayed similarities to context. There was great resistance to the presence of inner-city students. These schools were oriented towards achievement, and the students were constantly reminded of this orientation. Many faculty and parents thought that the reassignment of inner-city students to these schools was unnecessary. It was as if they were saying, "Why spread the problem of underachievement around? It is not my problem; it does not fall within my jurisdiction. Let somebody else take care of it." Thus the similar responses at Simpson and at Lincoln to the transferred students was based on similar orientations. There was fear that the students from the inner city would lower the schools' achievement ratings. There was constant reiteration of the achievement goals in these schools. In summary, many believed that the images of these schools would be tarnished, the academic standards hampered, and the teacher-student relationship upset.

Monroe and Highland, on the other hand, had different kinds of environments that were associated with different responses to the integration plan. These schools were not strictly achievement-oriented, although Highland has a reputation for being a fine institution. Essentially, Monroe and Highland were more flexible. While

Highland was administered in a democratic way, Monroe seemed to operate on a rather laissez faire philosophy. There were academic expectations but they were not stressed as much as at Lincoln and Simpson.

In particular, the principal and faculty at Highland were not concerned with image-building but with helping the students. Highland's experience with integrating physically handicapped and nonhandicapped students accounted for the ease with which it responded to the proposal to achieve racial integration.

As becomes apparent in the case of these four schools, we can better understand a school climate by examining the various influences exerted by the principal, faculty, students, and parents.

Administrators in each of the four schools exhibited definite patterns of leadership, and each pattern produced its effect upon integration. Simpson's principal maintained formal control of the policies and procedures that were carried out in the school. There were many rules, and they were strictly enforced. The principal was not hostile to reassigned inner-city children but she handled them in a firm way. The students and staff at Simpson knew what was expected of them, and the principal indicated to the new transfer students that they too must fit into the Simpson system. Thus some of the new students were given private lectures in addition to public scoldings and chidings when they got "out of line." The new children were made aware of the normative pattern in the school as quickly as possible. In the beginning of the year the principal's response toward the new black youngsters was "tense" and stern"; she did not know the youngsters, their brothers and sisters, or their parents; she did not know what to expect and was therefore uneasy in her relations with them. In the latter part of the year the principal began to relax, urging and cajoling the students to fulfill her expectations rather than admonishing them. The transfer children began to know the principal and to respond favorably to her expectations and to the normative pattern of the school. Their adjustment was made less difficult as the principal began to respond to each child individually rather than as "one of those Corliss children". During the second semester she began to address them by name, joke with them, and talk with many about their academic progress. The principal who had attempted to direct the new youngsters' adjustment by continually checking on their behavior finally relaxed and began to accept the new children; they, in turn, began to follow the rules.

Highland's principal gave leadership in deliberately planning for further integration. He emphasized a flexibile rather than a rigid approach. The principal's style of administering the school and relating to the students did not change with the arrival of a greater number of black students. His administrative orientation had always been one of participating with faculty and students in the operation of the school. He constantly urged the staff to guide and encourage the new children. He did not look upon the black students as potential behavior problems. He tailored discipline to the individual. What was perhaps most crucial for the new children's adjustment was the principal's awareness of what was actually happening in his school and his own recognition that as principal he was in a position to support the deliberate move toward integration by fostering an atmosphere of acceptance.

Lincoln Junior High School's principal was anxious about the integration plan. His style of leadership became more authoritarian as the year progressed. The Lincoln principal maintained a kind of militaristic stance against the new children, He was on guard and gave no quarter to the inner-city children transferred to his school. Emphasis was upon quick compliance with the administration's regulations. The students were controlled by threats and punishments which some of them believed to be unjust. The principal reiterated his views and policies throughout the year, saying, "These transfers obey the rules or else!" There was an uneasy feeling among the new students.

The Monroe Junior High School principal generated an entirely different kind of atmosphere. He led from afar in a laissez faire fashion. The principal was seldom seen talking with students in the halls or classes. Even discipline was not handled by the principal. Faculty members or the vice-principal handled most of the behavior problems. The transfer students, most of whom were white, were left alone. In general, they were on their own with little, if any, deliberate help in adjusting to Monroe. At times the school appeared to be without visible leadership. There was no observable planning on the principal's part to use his power and authority to make the integration process at Monroe either more or less difficult.

From the above analysis, it is clear that the most favorable school environment—that which contributed most to good education, racial integration, and pleasant working conditions for the teaching staff—was to be found at the Highland Elementary School. This environment was due, in part, to the school's history of caring for physically handicapped children. But more than this, it was due to the principal's attitude of acceptance and his leadership skill. This suggests that the principal's role is most important in establishing a school climate favorable to integration.

As we now see, the principal plays an important leadership role in helping to establish an educational environment that is favorable to learning and that fosters positive social relationships between students. Neither a threatening nor a laissez faire approach seem to be helpful. In Monroe, where the principal was aloof from the daily happenings in the school, neither he nor the faculty knew what students actually experienced at the school and how they really felt about the school. Our guess is that the discrepancy between faculty and student reactions to a predominantly black inner-city school is not limited to Monroe. The few extra services provided in some "higher horizons" schools like Monroe may fool the teachers but not the students.

Another important factor contributing to variations in assimilation is whether or not the student is new. When all four schools were combined, the assimilation self-ratings of students who were new neighborhood residents and those of reassigned or bused children were similar. The reassigned inner-city children, in general, felt assimilated into the new school about as much as new neighborhood residents. This is an important finding that resulted from the comparative analysis. In many studies of integration, investigators focus only upon the black or poor children and have no information on whether white or affluent children are having similar experiences. This, of course, is one of the weaknesses of noncomparative studies.

Teacher expectation is a third factor that fosters or impedes integration. Some teachers complained during the year that the transfer students, in particular the black children, were disruptive in class and a burden to both the other pupils and the teachers. These complaints were most frequently heard at Lincoln Junior High School and Simpson Elementary, the two schools with high academic reputations. Some faculty members at these schools tended to generalize from the behavior of a few students; if one black transfer student was troublesome then he or she began to symbolize for some teachers all of the transfer students. The data suggest that there were both black and white children among the troublemakers, but that for the most part students of both races adjusted well.

Several teachers responded differentially to disruptive behavior in students of different races. Thus, as one observer reported, a black transfer student at Lincoln was suspended for exactly the same behavior that had previously gone unpunished in a white neighborhood student.

On the other hand, several teachers used ingenious methods and techniques to involve new students in classroom activities. In many instances they avoided activities that involved one student choosing another to assist him. New students were usually left out of such activities since their names were not known to the old students. Some teachers singled out new students because of their disruptive behavior while other teachers singled out new students as models of good behavior.

In general, one might say that teachers of diversified student populations must be more sensitive if they are to be successful. In one school children were given morning milk if they paid a modest fee. The job of passing out the milk was assigned to a youngster from a low-income family whose parents could not pay for the milk. The teacher assigned the student this job as a way of involving him, but did not recognize the irony of having a milk attendant who could not drink the milk he passed out to others. This is an example of insensitivity, a problem frequently observed among teachers. A diversified student population cannot be successfully taught if the teachers have an attitude of "business as usual." Extraordinary planning and effort must be made to deal with the extraordinary circumstances and disparate experiences.

Teachers tend to feel that new neighborhood residents made better adjustments to a new school than inner-city bused students. The teachers persist in expressing this position, but we obtained similar self-ratings on assimilation from these two categories of pupils. This suggests that teachers are rating the white or affluent student in terms of an expectation that differs from the student's own experience. We conjectured that the favorable distortion of the adjustment of white children could cause resentment among black children. Poor adjustment behavior of blacks might be singled out because of their high visibility, while whites exhibiting similar behavior could be ignored because they were not expected to adjust poorly. Thus, the black youngsters would experience differential treatment not so much because the teacher misjudged their behavior, as is sometimes claimed, but because the teachers misjudged the behavior of their white or affluent classmates who may in fact have exhibited the same good or bad behavior as the black or low-income children.

In light of the above, we may conclude that people tend to react to situations in which they find themselves in terms of their system of beliefs. If teachers believe that white middle-income children assimilate better than black or low-income children, then these teachers tend not to notice the poorly adjusted behavior of some white children. The same teachers also tend not to notice the well adjusted behavior of some black children. The disprepancy in teachers' ratings of new neighborhood and reassigned students would appear to be a function of the stereotype.

We discovered that in addition to the school environment, which is created mainly by the attitudes and actions of the school professional personnel, the personal characteristics of the students had to deal with the new interpersonal experiences resulting from the bringing together of children of disparate backgrounds in a single school.

At the two junior high schools, the student's sex seemed to influence the integration process. Assimilation into a new school appeared to be easier for boys than for girls. In Monroe Junior High, for example, the white boys who had been transferred tended to follow the example set by the black boys who had attended Monroe the previous year. There was much interaction between the old students and the new white boys at Lincoln Junior High. They walked together to and from school and engaged in the usual hit-and-run play activities. However, the white girls at Monroe, which was predominantly black, were somewhat isolated. At the two elementary schools, which were predominantly white, both black boys and black girls tended to be "in the swing of things" by the end of the first semester.

7

OUR OVERALL FINDINGS
AS TO SOCIAL
ADJUSTMENT AND
SOCIOECONOMIC STATUS

We shall now analyze our findings and look again at the problems of the schools—first from the viewpoint of social adjustment and then from the viewpoint of economic status. The detailed facts and figures presented here should be more meaningful in light of the previous discussions; the earlier chapters can be said to have set the stage, and it has been enlightening to watch the actors—children, teachers, and principals—struggling to solve the complex problems.

The wisdom of analyzing assimilation ratings by students, teachers, and observers as three separate assessments rather than as a composite is revealed in a brief analysis of disagreements between these three. When all new students were considered, disagreements between the three raters ranged from a small difference of 7.6 percentage points between teachers and students on the number of students who were believed to have assimilated poorly to the highest difference of 18.6 percentage points between teachers and students in their assessments of the number of pupils who assimilated well (see Table 4 in the Appendix). Assessments by observers fell between these extremes. Thus the three raters agreed most in their judgments concerning which students assimilated poorly, and agreed least in their judgments concerning which students assimilated well. A principle that emerges is that it is easy for persons of different age levels, experience, and positions in society to reach a consensus on what constitutes failure or bad behavior, but difficult for them to agree in identifying desirable or good behavior. This study of the relativity in definition of assimilation is basic to the matter of understanding social adjustment. And it indicates that the perception and belief system of the observers, including teachers and principals, are important variables that must be reckoned with in assigning weight to their assessments of the social adjustment of others.

The following analysis is based upon 402 assimilation ratings provided by students new to the four schools, 591 ratings provided by observers, and 601 ratings provided by the students' homeroom teachers. Students' self-ratings were obtained at the end of the school year for only 61 percent of the study population. Observer ratings of students were obtained for 81 percent and faculty ratings for 90 percent of the study population. The low student response was due to administrative problems in testing and not to refusals on the part of the students, so the data are not biased by selective inclinations to participate in the study.

Students, teachers, and observers tended to agree most in their assessments of the assimilation of students reassigned to new schools to achieve racial balance; differences between any of the three ratings for reassigned students never exceeded 8 percentage points (see Table 4). The greatest agreement in the assessment of assimilation occurred between teachers and inner-city students. For example, the teachers thought that 63 percent of the reassigned students assimilated well, 23 percent moderately, and 14 percent poorly. The reassigned students, rating themselves on the extent to which they were liked by others or approved of their fellow students' behavior, revealed that 58 percent were well assimilated, 25 percent moderately assimilated, and 17 percent poorly assimilated. This rating pattern is very similar to that of the teachers.

The greatest difference in the assessment of assimilation occurred between white students and teachers; this discrepancy, however, had to do with the assimilation ratings for students new to a school because they had recently moved into a new school district and were, in effect, attending their "neighborhood school." Of students who had moved into a new school district, 58 percent considered themselves well assimilated, 27 percent moderately assimilated, and 16 percent poorly assimilated. These self-ratings are almost identical to those of the inner-city students new to a school because they had been reassigned by the School Board. This similarity suggests that newness itself is a variable in the social adjustment of children, and that it affected reassigned and new neighborhood children alike in this instance. While the teachers rated the assimilation of bused students in about the same way that these students rated themselves, the teachers were more liberal in their ratings of new neighborhood children who had recently moved into the school district. The teachers believed that 84 percent of the new neighborhood children had assimilated well, 11 percent moderately, and 5 percent poorly. The comparison of these ratings with those of the students themselves resulted in one of the largest discrepancies of ratings between students and teachers, students and observers, or teachers and observers.

75

Observers also tended to give better assimilation ratings to new neighborhood children than to children who had been reassigned to improve racial balance. However, discrepancies between observer and student ratings for these two categories of students were not as great as those between the teacher and student ratings. Of neighborhood children who were new to the four schools included in this study, observers considered 73 percent well assimilated, 18 percent moderately assimilated, and 9 percent poorly assimilated. But of inner-city children new because they had been reassigned by the School Board, observers believed 65 percent to be well assimilated, 15 percent moderately assimilated, and 21 percent poorly assimilated.

In summary, one might say that students, teachers, and observers made similar assessments of the assimilation pattern of reassigned students. Discrepancies are of the sort that might have occurred by chance: around 16.8 percent of the reassigned students thought that they had assimilated or adjusted poorly; the teachers concurred with this judgment, rating 14.4 percent of the transferees as poorly assimilated; and so did the observers, who gave 20.6 percent the lowest possible adjustment score. The three-way view of well-assimilated reassigned students followed a similar pattern: 58.4 percent of the students considered themselves well assimilated; the teachers considered 63 percent well assimilated; and the observers considered 64.6 percent well assimilated. The remaining proportion of students not reported here considered themselves moderately or poorly assimilated.

Two important findings grow out of the above analysis: (1) new neighborhood students and new bused students have similar reactions concerning the extent to which they accept and are accepted by other students; (2) teachers tend to rate as well assimilated more white middle-class neighborhood students than black inner-city reassigned students. The fact that most neighborhood students new to the four schools came from white and affluent families and that most reassigned students came from black and low-income families suggests that the teacher was rating the white student in terms of some expectation that differed from the student's own experience. It would appear, therefore, that the teacher's assessment of the black or low-income child from the inner-city was not so distorted as has been claimed in the past, but that the teacher's view of the white or affluent child from a middle-class neighborhood was impaired. Thus when the occasion for comparing children with different backgrounds arose, one did not recognize that the adjustment problems of the affluent and white were similar to those of the poor and black. This state of affairs could contribute to resentment among black youngsters. A black child might be singled out for poor behavior because of his high visibility in a predominantly white school and because the teacher expects him to be a poor assimilator, while the same behavior might go unnoticed in a white student.

This brief discussion of the findings confirms what is already known: People tend to consciously react in terms of their system of beliefs to the situation in which they find themselves. If teachers believe that white middle-class children assimilate better than black children from the inner city, these teachers tend not to notice the poorly adjusted behavior of some white children, even when the white children themselves insist that they are not doing well (15.5 percent of the new neighborhood children in this study indicated that they were poorly assimilated).

A general finding from this study that should be borne in mind is that an overwhelming majority of all new students—both the neighborhood residents and those reassigned by the School Board—felt they were moderately to well assimilated in the new schools they attended. This was the feeling of 84.5 percent of the new neighborhood residents and 83.2 percent of the new reassigned students.

The above has been an analysis of the assimilation patterns of all 656 new students considered in this study. What follows is a brief analysis of the assimilation of the new students in each of the two junior high and two elementary schools. Because the number of individuals involved is small—for example, only 14 of the new neighborhood students at Highland completed the Colvin Test given at the end of the year and only 17 reassigned students at Lincoln filled out the Hardt Student Opinion Test—this part of the discussion is limited to student and teacher responses but with no attempt to compare the two. (Table 5 gives the data for elementary and junior high schools.)

The school with the largest number of new students, 237, was Lincoln Junior High; the school with the lowest number, 108, was Highland Elementary. Simpson Elementary had 136 new students and Monroe Junior High had 175. The ratio of reassigned students to new neighborhood residents varied greatly among the four schools—reassigned students constituted 13.5 percent of the new students at Lincoln, 80.6 percent at Highland, 43.4 percent at Simpson, and 29.7 percent at Monroe. In general, the number of new students in the two junior high schools (401) was much larger than the number of new students in the elementary schools (241); but the proportion of new children who were new because they had been reassigned by the school board was smaller—only one-fifth in the junior high schools as compared with three-fifths in the elementary schools. New students were studied in grades one through three at Simpson, one through six at Highland, and seven through nine at Lincoln and Monroe. Since each of the four schools had more than 100 new students, a decision was made to proceed with plans to collect data that could be statistically analyzed. Because of the small numbers in some cells, such as the 21 new neighborhood residents at Highland and the 27 reassigned students at Lincoln, no sophisticated tests of significance were applied.

There was a notable difference between reassigned and neighborhood students at the two junior high schools. While half or more of the reassigned students at Monroe and Lincoln felt well assimilated, three-tenths or more (7 out of 24 for Monroe, and 6 out of 17 for Lincoln) felt that they were not doing so well and indicated that they were poorly assimilated. This means that they disliked most of the children in the school to which they were reassigned. Since most of the reassigned children at Lincoln were blacks and most of the reassigned children at Monroe were whites, race would appear not to affect the feelings of the reassigned children about their new school.

The assimilation pattern of children new to Lincoln or Monroe because their parents were new neighborhood residents varied greatly for each schools; moreover, the responses of these children were very different from those of the reassigned students in these two schools. While more than 60 percent (93 out of 143) of the new neighborhood students at Lincoln felt well assimilated into their new school, only 30 to 40 percent (27 out of 73) of the new neighborhood students at Monroe felt the same way. Also, 30 to 40 percent of the new neighborhood students at Monroe said they were poorly assimilated—this is the same as the proportion of students who felt well assimilated at Monroe. But the proportion of new neighborhood students at Lincoln who felt poorly assimilated into that school was much smaller, less than 10 percent (only 10 out of 143). The numbers are too small for an analysis that might result in a definitive statement, but it would appear that the reaction of the Monroe district residents to their "neighborhood school" was the reaction of ghetto dwellers to a slum school. In spite of the assertion of the Monroe School principal that the students preferred to attend that school, only 30 to 40 percent of the new black students at Monroe who lived in the inner-city neighborhood very much liked the other students who attended that predominantly black school. Thus, new residents of the Monroe area were not too pleased with their neighborhood school.

For the two elementary schools it is probably more profitable to analyze the teacher ratings, especially since the Colvin Picture Test was not given to students in all grade levels. Essentially, in Highland there was not much difference between the teacher's assimilation ratings of new neighborhood residents and reassigned students. Highland teachers considered nearly 70 percent (13 out of 19) of their new neighborhood children well assimilated, between 20 and 30 percent (5 out of 19) moderately assimilated, and only one of the 19 students poorly assimilated. On the other hand, Highland teachers rated more than 70 percent (64 out of 87) of the reassigned students as well assimilated, between 10 and 20 percent (13 out of 87) as moderately assimilated, and slightly more than 10 percent (10 out of 87) as poorly assimilated. Considering the small numbers involved, these variations are probably no more than chance occurrences.

Teachers at the Simpson Elementary School presented an entirely different picture. They saw a much higher proportion of new neighborhood residents than of reassigned students adjusting well to the school. Specifically, they thought that 80 to 90 percent (58 out of 68) of the new neighborhood residents were adjusting well, more than 10 percent (9 out of 68) of the new neighborhood residents were adjusting moderately, and only one of the 68 new neighborhood children was adjusting poorly. But Simpson teachers believed that only 40 to 50 percent (23 out of 52) of the reassigned children were well assimilated, that nearly 30 percent (15 out of 52) were moderately assimilated, and that nearly 30 percent (15 out of 52) were poorly assimilated. It should be pointed out, however, that the students at Simpson did not feel left out. In fact, nearly two-thirds of the reassigned students felt that they were well assimilated—that is, they believed they were well liked by other students. This was about the same as the proportion of new neighborhood residents who felt well liked.

The great discrepancy between the teachers' ratings of neighborhood students and their ratings of reassigned students would appear to be a function of the stereotype, although specific evidence was not available to nail down this assertion. Simpson is located in a middle-class section of the city and has a reputation for maintaining high standards. Many of the teachers and members of the PTA feared that the inner-city children to be bused to Simpson would lower the overall achievement rating of the school. They also believed that the inner-city children would not fit in. Hence, the teachers' low assimilation ratings of the reassigned children would appear to be a move in the direction of fulfilling their own prophecy.

Although Highland is located in a middle-class neighborhood and has many children with affluent backgrounds, the school has always been more heterogeneous in the racial and economic composition of its student population. Moreover, Highland has a great number of physically handicapped children. At one time it was the school to which most handicapped children were assigned. Highland, then, was accustomed to all sorts and conditions of children and graciously received all who came. The teachers at Highland made no prophesies about the reassigned children and thus had nothing to prove or disprove. New neighborhood residents and new reassigned children were not expected to behave differently. The absence of a differential expectancy at Highland probably accounts for the absence of a discrepancy in teachers' assimilation ratings for students in affluent and low-income families.

In spite of the teachers' ratings, it should be restated that most youngsters adjusted well to Highland and Simpson schools. Both are fine schools with good academic ratings. This is further evidence that the overall educational environment is the key to whether or not children like school at the elementary and secondary level.

We discovered something else about the school as a social system. Socioeconomic status plays an important role in our discussion of the social aspects of integration. It is sometimes said that the school is a reflection of the local community. This might be true if the local community referred to is the total community and not a specific neighborhood. If Simpson is a good school, it is not so much because the residents of the neighborhood want it to be that way as it is because the total community represented by the members of the Board of Education thinks that that particular neighborhood should have a good school. Likewise, school boards do not spend a disproportionate amount of the budget on inner-city schools, although inner-city action groups are constantly demanding that they do so.

The internal functioning of the schools was so inaccessible to the adult residents and the parents that in one particular neighborhood of the city a school boycott and a directive from the State Department of Education were required before the Board of Education would acknowledge that it had a responsibility to deliberately seek ways to overcome de facto segregated schools.

On the other hand, some parents in one neighborhood actively sought to defeat the proposal to transfer some inner-city children to schools in middle-class areas. They too had little effect upon the internal operation of the school. The inner-city children were transferred to the middle-class neighborhood and the children adjusted to the school in about the same way that new neighborhood children adjusted, in spite of the ruckus raised by some parents. This means that the school system has more authority and power than is acknowledged to restructure its operations to achieve the quality of education deemed desirable.

Analysis of student self-ratings in terms of socioeconomic status indicated that both new neighborhood and new reassigned students fitted in well with other students in all four schools, and that poor assimilators were found among all status levels in all schools (see Table 6). However, low-income status did tend to retard the assimilation of some children in these schools. But lower socioeconomic status had a negative effect upon the adjustment of less than one-third of the children from poorer families. So we may conclude that high socioeconomic status did not immunize students against poor social adjustment in school and that low socioeconomic status did not eliminate the possibility of very good social adjustment in various kinds of schools.

Students and teachers disagreed about the significance of race as a variable in assimilation (see Tables 9, 10, and 11). Teachers insisted that race made a difference in the assimilation of new students into a school. From the point of view of the students, however, race was not a significant variable and could not account for differential patterns of assimilation; neither could socioeconomic status, except among the very low income families where low status seemed to have a slight negative effect on the student's assimilation.

Throughout the analysis socioeconomic status and race have been alluded to as associated or not associated in one way or another with assimilation or social adjustment in school. It is time now to undertake a detailed analysis of these two variables and attempt to pin down the conditions under which they make a negative, positive, or neutral contribution.

The socioeconomic status of a student was inferred from the rating of the census tract in which his residence was located. Students' addresses were not systematically recorded but were available for about four-fifths of the 656 students in the study population. Specifically, 531 students were involved in this phase of the analysis.

All census tracts in the community have been classified here into five socioeconomic areas. They range from Area I, where many business and professional workers, most of whom are college graduates, live in expensive well-kept homes to Area V, where laborers, service workers, and semiskilled adults, most of whom have achieved only a grade school education or less, live in overcrowded and dilapidated dwelling units. Areas I, II, and III are above average and Areas IV and V are below average on most measures of socioeconomic status. Students in this study lived in all five socioeconomic areas. A majority of the students were about equally divided between either the highest or the lowest socioeconomic area. Areas I, II, III, IV, and V had 30 percent, 8 percent, 17 percent, 14 percent, and 31 percent of the students respectively. As previously stated, most of the students new to a school because their parents had recently moved into the school district were residents of Area I, and most of the students reassigned to a new school because of the proposal to improve racial balance were inner-city residents of Area V.

The first observation is that students of all socioeconomic levels fitted in well with the students at all four schools (see Tables 6, 7, and 8). A second observation is that students of all socioeconomic levels were found among those who were poorly assimilated in each of the four schools.

Among students who indicated the extent of their assimilation in school, there was no linear pattern of variation between assimilation and level of socioeconomic status. For example, 63.6 percent of all Area I students listed themselves as well assimilated but so did 62.5

percent of all Area IV students. Area I is above average and Area IV is below average on most measures of socioeconomic status. It is true that the Area V residents had the lowest proportion of students (51 percent) who felt that they were well assimilated. But this proportion was not much lower than the 55.6 percent of students in Area II who believed that they were well assimilated.

A modest indication that socioeconomic status made some contribution to the adjustment or assimilation of children in school was the fact that 36.3 percent of the Area V children were poorly assimilated. This proportion was twice as great as the 16.7 percent of youngsters in Area IV who were poorly assimilated and much greater than the 7 or 8 percent in Areas I, II, and III. So of the students who rated themselves on their degree of assimilation in school, only those who lived in the two below-average socioeconomic areas had a notable proportion who gave themselves negative or poor adjustment scores. It should be pointed out, however, that these students were far less than a majority of all new students who lived in below-average areas. The proportion of poor assimilators among students who rated themselves was never more than about one out of every three students.

A tentative conclusion, then, is that a very low socioeconomic status tends to impede the assimilation of some new children into a new school setting but has no effect upon most of the children. A further conclusion is that the majority of students, whether they have low or high socioeconomic status backgrounds, assimilate well in school—that is, they feel well liked by others and tend to approve of their schoolmates.

These tentative conclusions are corroborated by an analysis of the teacher and observer ratings, which tend to reveal patterns similar to those found in the student self-ratings. Teachers and observers felt that both poor and affluent students were well assimilated. While teachers thought that Area I residents had the highest proportion of well-assimilated new pupils, the proportion of Area I students they rated as well assimilated (88.4 percent) was not much greater than the proportion of Area III students rated similarly (84.4 percent). Moreover, the proportion of well assimilated students in Area II, which teachers listed as 76.9 percent, was less than the proportion in Area III. In the judgment of teachers and observers, the two below-average socioeconomic areas, IV and V, produced the highest proportions of poorly assimilated students. As was also indicated by the students' self-ratings, the proportion of poorly assimilated students among those living in Areas IV and V was twice as great as the proportion of such students living in the top three socioeconomic areas.

These data once more suggest the teachers' inclination not to expect poor assimilation from students with high-status families. While 8.1 percent of the students from Area I felt that they were poorly assimilated in their schools, and the observers thought that 6.1 percent of these students were poorly assimilated, the teachers rated only 3.2 percent of the high-status students as poorly assimilated. This inclination on the part of teachers, which was mentioned before, has implications for the kind of professional training they must have if they are to be effective in a pluralistic society.

While there is a slight tendency for below-average socioeconomic status to contribute to poor assimilation in school, the overall finding of this phase of the analysis is that high socioeconomic status does not immunize students against poor social adjustment in school and that low socioeconomic status does not eliminate the possibility of very good social adjustment in all kinds of schools. Both principles should be learned and remembered if we are to avoid the practice of responding in a stereotyped way to children of specific social classes. So the contribution of socioeconomic status to the assimilation of the student in school is modest. The educational environment provided by the school would appear to be a more significant variable for a majority of students of all status levels.

Yet the teachers persisted in believing that the lower-status reassigned children presented a greater number of problems than the higher-status new neighborhood residents (see Table 12). According to the teachers, problems in learning were found most frequently among the reassigned inner-city children. Teachers in all four schools judged that 65 percent of these children had learning problems, 41 percent had social interaction problems, and 62 percent had personality problems. In fact, teachers believed that 78 percent of the reassigned, lower-status, inner-city youngsters had one or more of the problems mentioned above; this is in spite of the similarity of these students' adjustment pattern with that of the mostly affluent new neighborhood residents, only 49 percent of whom were believed to be afflicted with personality, learning, or social interaction problems. The teachers reported that 41 percent of the new neighborhood residents had personality problems, 32 percent had problems in learning, and 22 percent had social interaction problems. As the teachers saw it, the poorer reassigned children presented personality, learning, or social interaction problems two or three times more often than the new neighborhood residents.

There was more divergence of opinion between students and teachers about race as a significant variable in school assimilation. We reached this conclusion after analyzing the various assessments of assimilation, according to categories of white and black students. All 656 students were involved in this analysis. About half of the students who were new to the four schools were black and about half were white. But the proportion of whites among new neighborhood students who lived near one of the four schools (three of which were located in middle-class areas) was vastly different from the proportion of whites among students reassigned to improve racial balance; 65 percent of the new neighborhood residents but only 28.3 percent of the reassigned students were white, whereas 35 percent of the new neighborhood residents and 71.7 percent of the reassigned students were nonwhite.

A majority of the reassigned students in three of the four schools were nonwhite—93.8 percent were nonwhite at Lincoln, 86.4 percent at Simpson, and 72.4 percent at Highland. Only in Monroe, the predominantly black school, was the majority of reassigned students white; but the number of black children among those reassigned to Monroe constituted a large minority (40.4 percent) considering that the goal of reassignment was to balance the black-white ratio. Neither did the small numbers of black students shifted to the other schools significantly increase the proportion of blacks in their student populations. The proportion of blacks in the three predominantly white schools was already increasing because families displaced by urban redevelopment tended to relocate in neighborhoods on the fringe of the inner-city area. The Lincoln and Highland school districts encompassed these fringe neighborhoods. Thus nearly 12 percent of new neighborhood children who entered Lincoln at the beginning of the school year were black and about 52 percent of the new neighborhood residents who entered Highland were black.

Because Simpson was located in a residential area that had not experienced much racial integration in housing, less than 7 percent (5 out of 77) of the new neighborhood students were black; this small proportion, together with the 45 black students reassigned to Simpson by the School Board and the few black families who already lived in the school district, raised the proportion of nonwhite students at Simpson to only about 5 percent. One might surmise from this analysis that the proposal of the School Board to reassign 314 black youngsters was not radical enough to improve the racial balance of those schools with high white-to-nonwhite ratios. The changes in racial balance that did take place in schools like Lincoln and Highland were due mainly to the residential mobility of the black families, a factor that was not controlled by School Board action.

In spite of this cautious and limited beginning, several parents groups, as mentioned earlier, vehemently resisted the integration plan. Their protests might be classified as excessive reaction to a minuscule change. The reactions of the students were different from those of their parents. To recapitulate, in the two elementary schools about the same proportion of new black inner-city residents as new white neighborhood students believed that other children at the new school liked them very much. A majority of the student population of both races felt this way.

84

While a majority of students in the two junior high schools felt accepted by their schoolmates, one-fifth of the new blacks were poorly adjusted. This proportion was almost twice as large as the proportion of new whites who had similar feelings. However, the larger proportion is not so much due to unhappy circumstances for the black students in the predominantly white school as it is a reflection of the displeasure that black youngsters new to the Monroe School neighborhood felt with their predominantly black junior high school located in the slums. When this special circumstance was removed from the analysis, the assimilation ratings that white and black junior high children gave themselves were similar, as seen in the analysis of all the elementary school children who attended schools outside of the slums.

Teachers insisted that race made a difference in the assimilation of new students into an existing school. One might recall that the teachers considered one-fifth of the new elementary school blacks to be poorly adjusted, which was twice as many as considered themselves to be poorly adjusted. Regarding white children who were new to the elementary schools, the teachers considered one-fifth to be poorly adjusted, which was half as many as considered themselves to be poorly adjusted. In summary, the teachers tended to view some black youngsters as less adjusted to the school setting than the students felt they were, and some white youngsters tended to feel less adjusted to the school setting than some teachers believed they were.

It was mentioned earlier that the principal of Monroe, the junior high school located in the inner-city area of Centralia, stated that the children who had been transferred to other schools preferred to attend Monroe. The students' reactions to their school in the slums were different from the assessment of their feelings given by the principal. Maybe he was only attempting to maintain the student population at an appropriate level so that the school would not be closed. Or it could be that the administrative and teaching staff have views of the school in which they work that differ from those of the students. More important, the school's professional personnel may not even be aware of differences between their perceptions of school and those of the students. The data of this study suggest this.

Seventy-five percent of the teachers at Monroe believed that the black youngsters new to the Monroe neighborhood were well as- similated, 15 percent believed that these students were moderately assimilated, and 10 percent believed they were poorly assimilated. The teachers' assumptions about the pattern of assimilation varied greatly from the feelings expressed by new black residents of the school neighborhood. Only 48 percent of these students felt well assimilated at Monroe, that is, less than half of the new black students approved of the behavior of their Monroe schoolmates and felt a part of the school; 28 percent felt poorly assimilated into the school, meaning that they disliked most of the other students or did not feel accepted by them. This discrepancy between the teachers' assessment of the Monroe School setting and that of the students is probably anchored in the different perspectives from which students and teachers view a school. The extra services and "higher horizons" programs, salary differentials, and other features that were innovated at the Monroe School probably changed the teachers' perceptions of that school but not the students'. Thus the principal's assertion that students preferred to attend Monroe may have been an honest statement of his expectation, but the students experienced the school as it was and were not pleased with what they experienced. This analysis further suggests that the teaching staff should be cautious in attempting to speak for the students. The students themselves must be heard.

In general, one might say that from the point of view of the students, race is not a significant variable accounting for differential patterns of assimilation and neither is socioeconomic status, except among very low-income families where a modest effect contributing to their poor assimilation was seen. From the point of view of teachers, however, both race and socioeconomic status are importantly related to the social adjustment of students in school. Teachers tend to believe that students from white and higher-status families adjust better and have fewer problems than students from black and lower-status families. From our point of view, it would appear that the educational environment of a school has a greater effect upon whether or not a student likes his school mates and feels he is accepted by them and is a part of the school than have personal characteristics and family circumstance.

In general, this study has confirmed what is known about the plasticity and adaptability of children. They do have more resilience than they are given credit for. The children in this study—from black and white families who lived in low-income and middle-class neighborhoods—accepted the challenge of a new school and environment. In most instances, they responded well and made favorable adaptations. The more difficult adjustment appeared to be that of the professional school personnel to the new circumstance of a racially and socioeconomically pluralistic student population. Unable to recognize, accept, and understand their own discomfort, some teachers and principals projected their uneasy feelings upon the students. This in turn aggravated the adjustment process.

When the school, through the leadership of its chief resident administrator, adopted a flexible and accepting posture, students were supported in their personal efforts to successfully adapt to the new situation. In such a surrounding, racial and socioeconomic factors were almost totally eclipsed in the minds of students and teachers as making any differential contribution to the social adjustment of bused and neighborhood children to the schools in which they were enrolled.

TABLE 1

New Area Residents or Reassigned Students
in Four Public Schools

	Total	
Student	number	percent
New neighborhood resident	426	64.9
Reassigned student	230	35.1
Total	656	100.0

TABLE 2

New Area Residents or Reassigned Students in Highland and Simpson Elementary and Lincoln and Monroe Junior High Schools

| | Elementary School | | | | Junior High School | | | |
| | Highland | | Simpson | | Lincoln | | Monroe | |
Student	number	percent	number	percent	number	percent	number	percent
New neighborhood resident	21	19.4	77	56.6	205	86.5	123	70.3
Reassigned student	87	80.6	59	43.4	32	13.5	52	29.7
Total	108	100.0	136	100.0	237	100.0	175	100.0

TABLE 3

Race of New Neighborhood Residents or Reassigned Students in Four Public Schools

| | New Neighborhood Resident | | Reassigned Student | | Total | |
Race	number	percent	number	percent	number	percent
White	277	65.0	65	28.3	342	52.1
Black	149	35.0	165	71.7	314	47.9
Total	426	100.0	230	100.0	656	100.0

TABLE 4

Assimilation Ratings of New Neighborhood
Residents and Reassigned Students by Students (Self-Rating), Teachers, and
Observers in Four Public Schools

	New Neighborhood Resident						Reassigned Student						Total					
	Student		Teacher		Observer		Student		Teacher		Observer		Student		Teacher		Observer	
Assimilation Rating	No.	%	No.	%	No.	%	No.	%	No.	%	No.	%	No.	%	No.	%	No.	%
1. Well assimilated	153	57.7	331	84.2	280	73.3	80	58.4	131	63.0	135	64.6	233	58.0	462	76.9	415	70.2
2. Moderately assimilated	71	26.8	42	10.7	69	18.1	34	24.8	47	22.6	31	14.8	105	26.1	89	14.8	100	16.9
3. Poorly assimilated	41	15.5	20	5.1	33	8.6	23	16.8	30	14.4	43	20.6	64	15.9	50	8.3	76	12.9
Total	265	100	393	100	382	100	137	100	208	100	209	100	402	100	601	100	591	100

TABLE 5

Assimilation Ratings of New Neighborhood Residents and Reassigned Students by Students (Self-Rating),
Teachers, and Observers in Two Elementary and Two Junior High Schools

	New Neighborhood Resident						Reassigned Student					
	Elementary			Junior High			Elementary			Junior High		
Assimilation Rating	Stu-dent	Tea-cher	Obser-ver	Stu-dent	Tea-cher	Obser-ver	Stu-dent	Tea-cher	Obser-ver	Stu-dent	Tea-cher	Obser-ver
Well	61.2	81.6	89.9	56.9	80.3	68.3	60.4	62.6	83.5	53.7	63.8	27.1
Moderately	30.6	16.1	10.1	25.9	12.0	20.5	29.2	20.1	11.5	14.6	27.5	21.4
Poorly	8.2	2.3	—	17.1	7.7	11.3	10.4	17.3	5.0	31.7	8.7	51.4
Total	100.0	100.0	100.0	100.0	100.0	100.0	100.0	100.0	100.0	100.0	100.0	100.0

TABLE 6

Percentage Distribution of New Neighborhood Residents and
Reassigned Students by Student Self-Ratings of
Their Assimilation and by Socioeconomic
Area of Student's Residence

Socio-economic Status of Student	Assimilation Rating by Student											
	New Neighborhood Students				Reassigned Students				Total			
	Well	Moderately	Poorly	Total	Well	Moderately	Poorly	Total	Well	Moderately	Poorly	Total
I	62.5	29.2	8.3	100.0	100.0	—	—	100.0	63.6	28.3	8.1	100.0
II	58.3	33.3	8.3	100.0	33.3	66.7	—	100.0	55.6	37.0	7.4	100.0
III	72.2	22.2	55.6	100.0	53.8	35.9	10.3	100.0	59.6	31.6	8.8	100.0
IV	64.7	11.8	23.5	100.0	61.3	25.8	12.9	100.0	62.5	20.8	16.7	100.0
V	36.8	22.8	40.4	100.0	56.4	18.2	25.5	100.0	51.0	12.7	36.3	100.0

TABLE 7

Percentage Distribution of New Neighborhood Residents and
Reassigned Students by Teachers Ratings of
Their Assimilation and by Socioeconomic
Area of Student's Residence

Socio-economic Status of Student	Assimilation Rating by Teachers											
	New Neighborhood Students				Reassigned Students				Total			
	Well	Moderately	Poorly	Total	Well	Moderately	Poorly	Total	Well	Moderately	Poorly	Total
I	88.8	7.9	3.3	100.0	75.0	25.0	—	100.0	88.4	8.4	3.2	100.0
II	81.8	12.1	6.1	100.0	50.0	33.3	16.7	100.0	76.9	15.4	7.7	100.0
III	82.4	14.7	2.9	100.0	79.4	10.3	10.3	100.0	84.4	12.0	7.6	100.0
IV	78.6	7.1	14.3	100.0	57.4	21.3	21.3	100.0	65.3	16.0	18.7	100.0
V	75.3	16.5	8.2	100.0	57.6	28.2	14.2	100.0	66.5	22.4	11.2	100.0

TABLE 8

Percentage Distribution of New Neighborhood Residents and
Reassigned Students by Observers' Ratings of
Their Assimilation and by Socioeconomic
Area of Student's Residence

Socio-economic Status of Student	Assimilation Rating by Observers											
	New Neighborhood Residents				Reassigned Students				Total			
	Well	Moderately	Poorly	Total	Well	Moderately	Poorly	Total	Well	Moderately	Poorly	Total
I	75.9	18.4	5.7	100.0	20.0	20.0	20.0	100.0	74.3	18.2	6.1	100.0
II	62.5	28.1	9.4	100.0	20.0	20.0	—	100.0	64.9	27.0	8.1	100.0
III	52.9	38.2	8.8	100.0	7.0	7.0	5.3	100.0	74.7	18.7	6.6	100.0
IV	64.3	10.7	25.0	100.0	15.9	15.9	9.1	100.0	72.2	13.9	13.9	100.0
V	84.7	5.9	9.4	100.0	18.7	18.7	35.2	100.0	66.7	11.8	21.5	100.0

TABLE 9

Percentage Distribution of Assimilation Ratings of New Neighborhood Residents and Reassigned Students by Student Self-Ratings and Ratings by Teachers and Observers and by Race of Students in Two Elementary Schools

Assimilation Rating

Three Kinds of Ratings by Race	New Neighborhood Residents				Reassigned Students				Total			
	Well	Moder-ately	Poorly	Total	Well	Moder-ately	Poorly	Total	Well	Moder-ately	Poorly	Total
Student												
White	60.5	31.6	7.9	100.0	55.0	30.0	15.0	100.0	58.6	31.0	10.4	100.0
Black	63.6	27.3	9.1	100.0	61.9	28.9	9.2	100.0	62.1	28.7	9.2	100.0
Teacher												
White	87.7	12.3	—	100.0	66.7	20.0	13.3	100.0	81.6	14.6	3.8	100.0
Black	50.0	35.7	14.3	100.0	61.5	20.2	18.3	100.0	60.2	22.0	17.8	100.0
Observer												
White	93.2	6.8	—	100.0	89.7	3.4	6.9	100.0	92.2	5.9	1.9	100.0
Black	75.0	25.0	—	100.0	81.8	13.6	4.6	100.0	81.0	15.1	3.0	100.0

TABLE 10

Percentage Distribution of Assimilation Ratings of New Neighborhood Residents and Reassigned Students by Student Self-Ratings and Ratings by Teachers and Observers and by Race of Students in All Four Schools

Assimilation Ratings

Three Kinds of Ratings by Race	New Neighborhood Residents				Reassigned Students				Total			
	Well	Moder-ately	Poorly	Total	Well	Moder-ately	Poorly	Total	Well	Moder-ately	Poorly	Total
Student												
White	63	28	9	100.0	51	27	22	100.0	61	28	11	100.0
Black	48	24	28	100.0	61	24	15	100.0	55	24	21	100.0
Teacher												
White	89	8	3	100.0	71	18	11	100.0	86	10	4	100.0
Black	75	15	10	100.0	60	24	16	100.0	67	20	13	100.0
Observer												
White	70	21	9	100.0	58	12	30	100.0	68	19	13	100.0
Black	79	13	8	100.0	67	16	17	100.0	73	14	13	100.0

TABLE 11

Percentage Distribution of Assimilation Ratings of New Neighborhood Residents and Reassigned Students by Student Self-Ratings and Ratings by Teachers and Observers and by Race of Students in Two Junior High Schools

Three Kinds of Ratings by Race	New Neighborhood Residents				Assimilation Rating Reassigned Student				Total			
	Well	Moderately	Poorly	Total	Well	Moderately	Poorly	Total	Well	Moderately	Poorly	Total
Student												
White	63.3	27.3	9.4	100.0	47.1	23.5	29.4	100.0	61.5	26.9	11.6	100.0
Black	42.2	28.9	28.9	100.0	58.4	8.3	33.3	100.0	45.8	24.3	29.9	100.0
Teacher												
White	89.3	7.0	3.7	100.0	76.9	15.4	7.7	100.0	87.8	8.0	4.2	100.0
Black	78.2	12.6	9.2	100.0	55.8	34.9	9.3	100.0	72.2	18.5	9.3	100.0
Observer												
White	60.8	26.7	12.5	100.0	25.0	21.4	53.6	100.0	55.9	26.0	18.1	100.0
Black	79.5	11.1	9.4	100.0	28.6	21.4	50.0	100.0	66.0	13.8	20.2	100.0

TABLE 12

Problems of New Neighborhood Residents or Reassigned Students as Seen by Teachers in Four Public Schools

Problems	New Neighborhood Resident		Reassigned Student		Total	
	Number	Percent	Number	Percent	Number	Percent
No personality, learning, or social interaction	184	51	44	22	228	40.7
Social interaction	3	1	1	1	4	0.7
Learning	21	6	21	10	42	7.5
Personality	42	12	17	8	59	10.5
Learning and social interaction	4	1	11	5	15	2.6
Personality and social interaction	13	4	8	4	21	3.7
Personality and learning	32	9	38	19	70	12.5
Personality, learning, and social interaction	59	16	62	31	121	21.6
Total	358	100.0	202	100.0	560	100.0

LaPorte, Robert, Jr., vii
Leadership, student, 55; in gym
  period, 56; patterns of various
  groups, 69
League of Women Voters, 16
Learners, slow, 26
Learning experience, 45; slow, 48,
  64; problems, 83
Librarian, opinion of, 49
Lipton, Aaron, 3, 8

Mass culture, white society, 4
Mays, Benjamin, 3
McCord, Arline Sakuma, 3, 6
Miller, S.M., 6
Mob, threatening, 2
Morgan, Perry, 5
Mothers Club, 13
Moynihan Report, 5

Negative concept, of blacks, 4
Negro children, control of destiny,
  2
Neighborhood schools, 11, 15, 16;
  busing problems of, 35; minority
  groups in, 63
Neighborhood students, friendli-
  ness of, 32; middle-class, 46;
  assimilation of new residents,
  71; comparison of ratings, 75-76;
  reaction studied, 78
Newspaper, school, 66

Observers, classroom, 11, 20, 21,
  26, 30, 32, 35; lack of security
  because of, 35, 39, 47, 48, 58;
  and faculty rating, 75; assessment
  of assimilation problems, 75;
  analysis of ratings, 82-83
Open school policy, 16, 17

Parents, reactions of, 11, 25, 34-
  35, 37; types, 39, 48; integration,
  58; and resistance to integration,
  84

Parent-teacher associations, 16,
  19, 26, 35, 48; reaction to
  busing, 79
Peterson, A. D. C., 6
Pettigrew, Thomas, 3, 8
Playground observations, 40-42
Population study, 81
Powell, Gloria Johnson, 4
Prejudices, general, 7
Principals, role of, 11, 17, 20, 25,
  26, 32-33, 35-37; leadership,
  45; attitude, 47-48, 51; prejudice
  charge, 53; policy, 57, 66, 68;
  patterns of leadership in four
  schools, 69-70; perception as
  to social adjustment, 74; view of
  transference, 85; related to
  student perception, 86; adjustment to pluralistic student
  population, 86
Protest groups, 13
Psychological adjustment, 2
Punishments, unjust, 70

Race, mixing, 2, 3, 4; as a variable,
  13, 14; teacher attitude, 30; homogeneous to heterogeneous groups,
  67; achieving integration, 67;
  housing, 84
Racial balance, problems in schools,
  11, 13, 14-15, 16, 17, 18, 19, 25;
  alleviation of imbalance, 35, 46;
  groupings, 49; as beginning of
  integration process, 67; plans to
  improve, 75-76; different proportions of, 84; improvement of,
  84
Racial identification, 4; segregation, 12; discrimination, 12
Racial superiority, claim of whites,
  5
Reading, remedial, 30; skills, 30;
  emphasis on, 39; case of one
  problem, 61
Reassignment scheme, 15; assimi-

lation problems, 75
Relevancy, definition of, 6
Research Department, 12
Roby, Pamela, 6
Ryan, Margaret, 7

School boards, role played by,
13-16, 16, 20, 25, 26, 34, 37, 58,
80
School environment, importance of,
70; inner-city problems of, 71;
added factors, 72
Schools, problems of racial balance,
11; crowded conditions of, 12;
de facto segregation of, 13; host
or receiving, 25; inner-city, 15,
17; freedom in, 32; adjustment
to new students, 34; keeping of
standards, 36; climate of, 45;
transfer from inner-city, 46;
lower-class youth to middle-
class school, 67; lower-class
students shut out of informal
groups, 67; transfer students
might tarnish school image, 68;
study of staff and student leadership in four schools, 69
Seeley, John, 1
Segal, Phyllis, 5
Segregation, official sanction of,
4; Supreme Court decision outlawing enforced, 4; as to open
school policy, 17; overcoming
de facto segregated schools, 80
Self-concept, 4, 26
Self-evaluation, 3; and self-awareness, 4
Sickels, Dorothy, vii
Social adjustment, 1-2; of elementary school students, 11; of
junior high school students, 11;
newness as a variable in, 75; in
reassignment, 79; poor and good
analysis of, 83
Social change, extent of, 5, 15

Social class, stereotyped by, 83
Social scientists, black and white,
6
Social structure, reform of, 6;
newness an important variable
in, 67, 68; interaction problems
of, 83
Social workers, 51, 53
Socioeconomic status, lowest and
above-average, 15, 24; lower,
25, 45, 46; low, 58; family
income, 58; different levels of,
67, role of, 80; self-rating by,
80; influence on good or poor
social adjustment, 80; relation
to assimilation, 81-82; related
to new children, 82; race as a
variable, 86
State Department of Education,
messages of, 14, 80
State Human Relations Commission,
14
Stereotyped opinions of blacks, 48
Stern, George, 7
Student body, dwindling, 17; new,
29; behavior problems, 31;
ignoring of new, 38; differential
treatment of, 51; injustice suffered by, 51-52
Student groups, ability, 39; reading,
39; involvement of new students
in activities, 71; self-rating, 75;
new students feel well assimilated,
77; variations in reassignment,
77; new student data studied,
77-78; poor adjustment scores,
82; self-rating patterns, 82;
opinion as to race problems, 83;
perspectives differing from those
of teachers, 86
Students, courage of, 2, low-achieving, 15; inner-city, 15; new ones
ostracized, 63; acceptance of old
by new, 62
Superintendents, influence of, 13-15,

16, 20, 26, 47-48
Supreme Court; Brown v. Board
   of Education, 4
Syracuse University Youth Development Center, vii

Tardiness, 38
Teacher-pupil ratio, 26
Teacher ratings, analysis of, 78;
   discrepancy in, 79
Teachers, attitudes of, 5, 11, 25-
   30, 36; as a creative group, 38;
   orientation of, 45; case study by,
   49, 51; attitude towards black
   students, 53; only black teacher
   in a school, 56; bypassing
   transfer students, 61; establishing order, 61, 66; teacher-
   student relationships, 68, 71;
   expectations of, 71; insensitivity
   of, 72; perception as to social
   adjustment, 74; assimilation
   ratings by, 75; views on adjustment problems of white and black
   students, 77; analysis of teachers'
   ratings, 82; view as to race, 83,
   85; difference between teacher
   and student perceptions, 85, 86
Transfer Program, problems of,
   16, 19, 49; students as class
   leaders, 53; disruptive actions,
   60; bypassed by teachers, 61;

isolation of groups, 64; various
   attitudes of transferred students,
   64; similar responses to, 68
Troublemakers, student, 17, 48,
   51, 71

Urban renewal, and inner-city
   schools, 17; problems of redevelopment, 84

Verbal expression, deficiency in,
   31

Walsh, Mary, vii
White children, social skill
   development of, 3; in race mixing, 3; assigned to new school,
   20; transferred, 46; problems of
   new students, 54; withdrawal
   from activities, 59; mixing with
   blacks, 62; rejection of one in a
   black school, 63; middle-class
   adjustment of, 72; new to
   school, 85
Whites, with children in integrated
   schools, 2; position of dominance,
   4; less able to impute inferiority
   to blacks, 5; opposing student
   transfer, 16; influence in reassignment problems, 76
Williams, Robin, 7

ABOUT THE AUTHORS

CHARLES V. WILLIE is Vice President for Student Affairs and Professor of Sociology at Syracuse University. He is a fellow of the American Sociological Association and a member of the Board of Directors of the Social Science Research Council. President-elect of the Eastern Sociological Society, Dr. Willie will serve as president in 1974-75. He is a member of the Panel on the Benefits of Higher Education of the Human Resources Board of the National Research Council.

Dr. Willie has written and edited several books including Black Students at White Colleges (with Arline Sakuma McCord), Racism and Mental Health (with Bernard Kramer and Bertram Brown), and The Family Life of Black People.

Dr. Willie was born in Dallas, Texas, and has attended segregated and integrated schools, colleges and universities. He received an A.B. degree from Morehouse College, an M.A. degree from Atlanta University, and a Ph.D. degree in Sociology from Syracuse University.

JEROME BEKER is Director of the Department of Studies in Child Care at the Institute for Child Mental Health in New York City. He is also Editor of Child Care Quarterly.

Dr. Beker has published widely in fields related to the education and mental health of children and adolescents. He has written two books as well as chapters in a variety of others, and his articles and reviews have appeared in the Journal of Educational Psychology, Integrated Education, the Journal of Negro Education, Urban Education, Psychology in the Schools, Criminology, and others.

Dr. Beker holds a B.A. degree from Swarthmore College and an M.A. and an Ed.D. from Teachers College, Columbia University.

DEADLOCK IN SCHOOL DESEGREGATION:
A Case Study of Inglewood, California
                    Edna Bonacich and Robert F. Goodman

BUSING: THE POLITICAL AND JUDICIAL
PROCESS
                    James Bolner and Robert Shanley

POLITICAL SOCIALIZATION OF CHICANO
CHILDREN
A Comparative Study with Anglos in California
Schools
                    F. Chris Garcia

BLACK STUDIES IN PUBLIC SCHOOLS
                    Raymond H. Giles, Jr.

SCHOOL BOARDS AND SCHOOL POLICY:
An Evaluation of Decentralization in New
York City
                    Marilyn Gittell, with Maurice Berube,
                    Boulton H. Demas, Daniel Flavin,
                    Mark Rosentraub, Adele Spier, and
                    David Tatge

BLACK TEACHERS IN GHETTO SCHOOLS:
A Case Study of Washington, D.C.
                    Catherine Bodard Silver

EVALUATING SCHOOL BUSING:
Case Study of Boston's Operation Exodus
                    James E. Teele

BLACK STUDENTS AT WHITE COLLEGES
                    Charles V. Willie and Arline Sakuma
                    McCord